A PRACTICAL GUIDE TO
COMPLEX PTSD

A PRACTICAL GUIDE TO
COMPLEX
PTSD

Compassionate Strategies to
Begin Healing from Childhood Trauma

ARIELLE SCHWARTZ, PHD

callisto
publishing
an imprint of Sourcebooks

Copyright © 2020 by Callisto Publishing LLC
Cover and internal design © 2020 by Callisto Publishing LLC
Copyright page credit: Illustration ©iStock/ Galina Shafran, cover.
Interior and Cover Designer: Michael Cook
Art Producer: Tom Hood
Editor: Seth Schwartz
Production Manager: Michael Kay
Production Editor: Ruth Sakata Corley

Published by Callisto Publishing LLC C/O Sourcebooks LLC
P.O. Box 4410, Naperville, Illinois 60567-4410
(630) 961-3900
callistopublishing.com

Printed and bound in China
OGP 2

I dedicate this book to those of you who have suffered from abuse or neglect as children and to the caring individuals who walk with you on your healing path. May the words and practices offered in this book provide guidance and inspire you with hope.

Contents

Introduction

When we imagine the birth of a child, any child, we see a world that is safe. We envision a home filled with kindness and nurturance. While this home may not be perfect, it is a place where a child is able to learn and grow with curiosity and joy. Childhood trauma is a betrayal of this unspoken promise.

Complex post-traumatic stress disorder (C-PTSD) is a response to traumatic events that were ongoing or repeated. With childhood trauma, these events occurred in your early years and were likely to be unpredictable, chaotic, or terrifying. You may have had parents or caregivers who abused, neglected, or abandoned you repeatedly, or you may have seen repeated traumatic events. The "complex" aspect of C-PTSD means that the trauma was at an early enough age or was repeated often enough that it affected your emotional development.

Alternatively, you might be a spouse, caregiver, friend, or therapist who is reading this so that you can provide support for someone who suffered from childhood trauma. In either case, this book will serve as a guide for the healing journey.

This book is meant to provide compassionate support in the process of healing from childhood trauma. You can think of it as a lantern that will illuminate dark spaces and provide a sense of hope in moments of despair. As a psychologist who

specializes in the treatment of childhood trauma and C-PTSD, I know the courage it takes to walk this path. I also know from experience that healing is possible. My own journey of healing from childhood trauma led me to specialize my therapy practice on the treatment of PTSD. I quickly discovered that clients were rarely coming to therapy with single traumatic events and that they did not respond quickly to treatment. Many of these clients had been misdiagnosed, felt frustrated with therapy, and were seeking a therapist who was willing to think outside the box when it came to treatment. Over the past 20 years, I have spent much of my career focusing on the most effective therapeutic interventions for complex trauma recovery.

The practical strategies you will learn in this book are taken from the most effective therapeutic interventions for trauma recovery. You will learn the skills to improve your physical and mental health by attending to the painful wounds from your past without feeling flooded with overwhelming emotion. My wish is to help you discover a new sense of freedom. The traumatic events of your past no longer need interfere with your ability to live a meaningful and satisfying life.

There are several ways you might approach this book. You might choose to read it on your own to help you understand

the process of healing. However, most often, the deep work of reclaiming yourself from the grips of childhood trauma will be most powerful when it is a collaboration between you and a caring, trauma-informed therapist who can provide much-needed acceptance for the parts of you that feel unlovable, damaged, shameful, or unworthy. Together with a caring supporter, you can walk this healing path.

The guidance offered in this book can provide valuable support between therapy sessions and help you feel secure in your own capacity to turn toward yourself lovingly and compassionately. It's important to note, though, that recovery from C-PTSD is rarely achieved in short-term therapy. If you expect therapy to be a quick fix, you are likely to feel disappointed. Keep in mind that healing will take time. Be patient with yourself and with anyone you turn to for support and guidance. If you have not yet found a therapist you can trust or you do not know where to seek support, turn to the end of this book to find a list of resources to support your healing journey.

You might also choose to work through this book with a spouse or caring friend alongside. When choosing to share your experience with another person, it is wise to look for someone who is invested in listening to you nonjudgmentally and in understanding your unique life experiences. You may choose to read passages aloud that resonate with you, or you might write down your reflections and then read these aloud. If you do choose to share your experience, take your time to

notice how it feels to be witnessed by another. I invite you to slow down enough so that you can sense and feel your body and your emotions. Remember, you get to choose whether, when, how much, and with whom you share the sacred truths of your inner world.

I recommend that you work through the book at a pace that allows you to digest the material you are reading. Throughout, you will have opportunities to read stories about other people's experiences with C-PTSD. These client stories are composites of several real-life cases in which all identifying information has been changed to protect the privacy and anonymity of the people involved. These stories might feel relatable or connected to your own past, and so they might evoke vulnerable emotions. If, at any point, you notice yourself becoming activated or triggered—in other words, you begin to feel overwhelming emotions—I invite you to see this as a signal to pause and reflect. Rather than pushing past your discomfort, I suggest you use this time to become curious. Ask yourself what you need in order to feel supported before you move on through the book.

We will start our exploration of C-PTSD by looking at what it is, what the symptoms are, and what causes it. The remaining chapters will cover the most common types of symptoms, including the avoidant, invasive, and depressive. The book will look at important skills for healing from emotion-regulation issues and interpersonal problems.

We will also explore common ways that C-PTSD interferes with everyday functioning, from hijacking our consciousness to undermining our sense of self-worth. Each chapter will include story examples, as well as practical tools and techniques you can use to cope with trauma and reclaim your life.

If you are looking for specific healing techniques, turn to the index in this book to find information on any method you're interested in. You can use any of these coping strategies at any time.

An important note: C-PTSD can be caused by any sort of trauma experienced in childhood, including growing up in an area affected by war and other violence or by seeing or experiencing human trafficking and child exploitation. While the healing strategies offered in this book will be of benefit to you no matter what form of trauma you have faced, the discussion on these pages will primarily focus on childhood trauma from parents, caregivers, family members, or community members.

It is important to remember that you cannot rush the healing process. It takes approximately 20 years for the human brain to fully form and many years of careful guidance for a child to develop the social and emotional intelligence to navigate the complexities of adulthood. Our earliest years should prepare us for the inevitable challenges of life, such as working through conflicts with loved ones or coping with loss. However, when you have grown up with childhood trauma, you have to fill in the gaps left behind by neglect or abuse,

and this process takes time. I encourage you to recognize that reclaiming your life from childhood trauma requires a long-term commitment to yourself and to the healing process. Your symptoms are the result of traumatic injuries that occurred over an extended period. It is important to be realistic about the timeline for healing.

In time, it is possible to reclaim a secure sense of self. Each tender moment of growth stretches your body, mind, and soul. Initially, you might feel shaky and unsure. Like a child just learning to walk, you may falter as you explore new territory. But with encouragement, you can get up again and again. With practice, you will develop greater faith in your capacity to sustain a positive mindset and a hopeful outlook toward your future. Remember, these hard-earned insights and experiences of empowerment cannot be taken from you. Eventually, you will reach a tipping point of growth at which you no longer identify with the shame and burdens of your childhood wounds. You can let go of the pain; you can learn to stand with unshakable confidence in the basic goodness of who you are, with the knowledge that you not only deserve it but also that it is the inexorable birthright of all human beings.

1

Understanding Complex PTSD

Childhood trauma has a profound impact on the body and mind, and this carries into adulthood. As a survivor, you might hold beliefs that you are damaged, that you are not lovable, or that you cannot trust anyone. You might have feelings of shame, unworthiness, or helplessness. Perhaps you feel plagued by anxiety or believe that you don't belong in this world. These kinds of thoughts and feelings might lead you to withdraw from relationships in order to avoid further rejection or hurt. Or, you might use food, alcohol, or drugs to disconnect from or numb yourself to the pain. If you relate to these symptoms, it is important to know that you are not alone. The painful emotions of complex PTSD are remnants of your past. More importantly, you *can* heal.

Surviving Childhood Trauma

Often, complex trauma begins in infancy. Infants are completely dependent upon their caregivers to help them feel safe, connected, and calm. Growing up with parents who were unpredictable, abusive, or neglectful shapes a child's vulnerable nervous system. This can lead to long-lasting patterns of emotional and physiological distress that the child then carries into adulthood. Memories of physical or sexual abuse can bring up strong emotions and evoke bodily sensations that a person may find hard to put into words and which can be difficult to understand. For instance, you may have memories that are unclear, which can in turn give rise to feelings of self-doubt. When traumatic events remain unhealed, it is common to replay these events in your mind as recurrent memories, flashbacks, nightmares, or disturbing feelings that invade your current life and relationships. Moreover, your ability to care for yourself as an adult is often a reflection of how well you were cared for as a child.

Healing from C-PTSD often requires a positive relationship with a therapist who fully accepts you for who you are and helps you reclaim your trust in other people. However, there are many steps you can take on your own. The healing strategies in this book are designed to help you reduce anxiety, helplessness, and shame. In time, you can develop your capacity to compassionately and nonjudgmentally accept yourself, which will help you make the essential shift from mere survival to thriving. You *can* reclaim your life from the suffering of childhood trauma.

ISABELLA

"I'm just too complicated to love"

Isabella came into our session feeling emotionally cut off and shut down. She had difficulty making eye contact. She collapsed into the couch and said that she was in "that place of nothingness." At this point in her therapy, we both understood that these words were her way of saying she was feeling dissociated—disconnected from her emotions and sensations. "The nothingness protects you from feeling the pain, doesn't it?" I said. She nodded.

Slowly, we began to explore whether there had been an event that might have triggered the dissociation. After some conversation about it, Isabella shrugged her shoulders and said, "I did have a fight with my husband." I invited her to tell me more about the fight, supporting her in opening up to some of the feelings that had been too much to handle at the time.

She said, "It was a bad one; we were both so angry. We said things that we both regret. I think he's really going to leave me this time. I'm just too much of a burden with all my trauma. I'm just too complicated to love!" While she felt too embarrassed at first to admit it, Isabella eventually shared that, after the argument with her husband, she had had a few drinks because she didn't have the resources to cope with the distress. She woke up the next day feeling foggy and tired. Now, she felt numb.

I knew that Isabella had grown up rejected by her mother and abandoned by her father. As we talked about the fight, we connected her early abandonment experiences to her fear that her husband would leave her. Together, we tuned into the young part of her that had felt those original losses of connection. We made space for the part of her that felt like a burden and allowed that part to be included in her present-moment experience.

Over the next several minutes, the "nothingness" began to subside, and even though Isabella felt sad, she also felt relieved. She began to look around the office and eventually she made eye contact with me. She described feeling more connected to herself. I asked how things were with her husband since the fight. She said, "He's actually been really nice to me, but I've been pushing him away. I've been holding the fight against him. When I dissociated, I was also shutting him out. I can stop doing that now."

C-PTSD Explained

At some point in our lives, most of us will experience at least one highly stressful or traumatic event, whether this is the unexpected loss of a loved one, a life-threatening accident, an act of violence, or a natural disaster. It is normal to feel afraid, shaky, confused, sad, or angry after these types of events. Ideally, we have support—through caring family, partners, friends, support professionals, or community members—to work through these emotions. However, if we do not have the resources to cope with a threatening or horrific event, these psychological and physiological responses to trauma can persist and develop into post-traumatic stress disorder (PTSD).

There are three main categories of PTSD symptoms: re-experiencing, avoidance, and pervasive feelings of danger. *Re-experiencing* symptoms include intrusive memories and flashbacks, or nightmares that are accompanied by strong emotions or sensations. *Avoidance* symptoms refer to the way you might avoid going to places, participating in activities, or seeing people who are associated with the traumatic event. You may engage in addictive behaviors, such as drinking too much or using drugs, in order to avoid thinking about the past. *Pervasive* feelings of danger might lead you to feel as though you are still being threatened, when you are actually safe. This is called "hypervigilance," and it can lead you to startle easily or feel on guard and unable to relax.

In contrast, complex PTSD (C-PTSD) occurs as a result of repeated or ongoing events. While C-PTSD can arise at any point in life, this book focuses on childhood trauma, such as growing up within an environment of fear, chaos, rejection, and abandonment. If you are reading this book, you may have experienced abuse, neglect, exposure to domestic violence, abuse from a sibling, or relentless bullying with no one to protect you. C-PTSD often arises from events that were both threatening and unescapable, though it can also be a result of ongoing emotional neglect, during which time you were chronically rejected or left alone for extended periods. Often this lack of nurturance from loving caregivers is coupled with inadequate protection from dangerous situations or people.

According to the World Health Organization's International Classification of Diseases (ICD-11), a diagnosis of C-PTSD includes the symptoms of PTSD, but also has three additional categories of symptoms: difficulties with emotion regulation, an impaired sense of self-worth, and interpersonal problems. C-PTSD is associated with intrusive flashbacks, feelings of panic, overwhelming feelings of rage, debilitating feelings of hopelessness, chronic feelings of shame, a harsh and unrelenting "inner critic," and a lack of trust in other people.

The most important thing to know about the symptoms of C-PTSD is that they are *learned* behaviors that can be unlearned with practice. Childhood trauma is *relational* trauma, which means that the wounds have to do with how we connect to others. New learning and growth is often best supported in the context of therapy. Within this healing relationship, you can experience reparative relational experiences while building new, healthy coping strategies.

Attachment Theory

The first three years of our lives are the attachment phase of development. During this time, we learn how to respond to the world and the people in it. In order to develop healthy interpersonal skills, we need to feel safe and secure in our relationships with our parents and other primary caregivers. This allows us to develop a healthy sense of self that forms the foundation for our ability to maintain meaningful, strong relationships as adults.

Children respond to these earliest relationships by developing attachment styles based on their inborn temperament, as well as their experiences with caregivers. Let's take a closer look:

Secure attachment: This style forms when a primary caregiver is predictable, consistent, and trustworthy. Your parents did not have to be perfect, and times of disconnection or misunderstanding are inevitable. However, a "good enough" parent provides opportunities to repair moments of disconnection, which builds your capacity to handle stress. A child who feels securely attached sees their parent as a source of comfort and feels comfortable exploring, learning, and playing because they know they have a safe place to come home to. As an adult, this security translates into the ability to develop meaningful connections with others while skillfully handling inevitable conflicts.

Insecure ambivalent attachment: This style arises when a primary caregiver was inconsistent and unpredictable. There may have been times in which you felt cared for, but these times were interspersed with experiences of being yelled at or rejected for expressing your needs. These mixed messages typically lead to feelings of uncertainty because you could not trust that a loving and caring parent would be there when you needed him or her. In adulthood, those with an insecure ambivalent attachment style may feel fearful about being abandoned, while also feeling strongly dependent on significant people in their lives, especially romantic partners.

Insecure avoidant attachment: Here, a primary caregiver was disengaged, distant, and unavailable. Typically, the caregiver dismissed or ignored your needs to be loved, accepted, seen, and understood. As a result, you learned to take care of your own needs by becoming independent and self-reliant. In adulthood, if you have an insecure avoidant attachment style, you may have a dismissive attitude toward your own emotions, as well as those of others. As a result, you might struggle with intimacy, especially when your partner desires a deeper connection.

Disorganized attachment: This attachment style arises when a primary caregiver was chaotic and abusive. Instead of being a source of love and care, the parent was a source of terror. Because we have an innate, biological drive toward attachment, children still attach to parents who are aggressive and cruel perpetrators of abuse. There is an inherent double bind between our inborn need for closeness and the equally strong need to escape danger. Over time, this unsolvable dilemma leads to feelings of helplessness and hopelessness. In adulthood, if you have a disorganized attachment style, you might alternate between feeling high-arousal emotions of fear, irritability, or anger and low-arousal emotions of defeat, despair, or depression. It is also common to repeat the relational patterns you learned in childhood by partnering with people who are abusive or by behaving abusively yourself.

Most of us develop a combination of attachment strategies, in part because we may have had more than one parent who may have treated us differently.

The important thing to know is that you can develop what attachment experts call "earned secure attachment," in which you learn how to feel securely attached in adulthood even if your caregivers didn't teach you. An essential part of this learning is to recognize the impact of childhood events on your sense of self. The ability to coherently and accurately talk about your past is a sign of earned security. Understanding your attachment problems allows you to practice reaching out for support from others and, increasingly, to tolerate authentic connection. This self-awareness can also help you success-fully repair situations when you have misunderstood or hurt a loved one.

Emotional and Physical Symptoms

This section introduces you to the more common symptoms of C-PTSD. We will go into greater depth about each category of symptoms in the chapters that follow, but this is a brief explanation:

Avoidance symptoms: Avoidance involves behaviors that disconnect you from painful, traumatic memories and uncomfortable sensations or emotions. You might stay away from places or people that remind you of the past. Or, you might withdraw from these social situations or use substances to push away the pain.

Invasive and intrusive symptoms: Often referred to as re-experiencing, invasive or intrusive symptoms interfere with your ability to feel safe and relaxed. In some cases, you might have clear memories of trauma that arise as nightmares or flashbacks. In other cases, you might feel flooded by emotions or by uncomfortable feelings in your body owing to traumatic events that happened when you were very young. One of the challenges of all types of post-traumatic stress is feeling like you are being threatened when you are actually safe. These pervasive feelings of danger can cause hypervigilance—being highly sensitive to sounds and sights in your environment.

Depressive symptoms: Often the anxiety of invasive symptoms alternates with that of depressive symptoms, in which you feel "shut down" and heavy. When there is no way to escape repeated emotional or physical abuse, children begin to feel powerless and ineffective. The feeling that nothing can or will ever change may be pervasive and dominate your worldview.

Difficulties with emotion regulation: Childhood trauma and attachment wounds can lead you to feel emotionally unstable, especially if you have felt abandoned, rejected, threatened, or out of control. You might often feel overcome by irritability, anger, or rage. Without help, such emotional suffering can develop into urges to hurt yourself or others.

Dissociative symptoms: Dissociative symptoms are some of the most debilitating experiences among C-PTSD survivors. Dissociation is both a psychological and a physiological survival mechanism. For example, a child who is dependent upon abusive caregivers needs to make this dangerous event tolerable, even if only in fantasy. A child may create an idealized mommy or daddy to avoid facing the reality of the external world. Physiologically, dissociation involves neurochemicals that numb feelings and sensations, leaving you feeling foggy, dizzy, nauseous, and tired. Sometimes, dissociation makes it difficult or impossible to remember traumatic events, which can lead to further disorientation.

Interpersonal problems: Attachment issues tend to interfere with your ability to form healthy relationships in adulthood. It can be difficult to trust or feel close to others. You might feel overly dependent and have difficulty asserting yourself in relationships. Or you might have developed an opposite pattern of becoming overly self-reliant, whereby you falsely believe you cannot depend upon anyone and, as a result, you push loved ones away unnecessarily.

Self-perception issues: Complex trauma is associated with an impaired sense of self-worth. Experiences of abuse or neglect often lead to self-blame. When you cannot stop a parent from drinking or protect a sibling from abuse, you might start believing that you are powerless, that you are worthless, or that the world is untrustworthy. You might carry toxic shame, in which you believe you are at fault, damaged, unworthy, or a failure. Over-identification with these negative beliefs forms a distorted sense of self.

Distorted thoughts and feelings about an abuser: Sometimes, C-PTSD survivors feel immense confusion about relationships with abusive caregivers. For example, you might feel guilt or sadness as you consider whether to stay in a relationship with an abusive parent. Or, you may feel acutely aware of the fact that your parent faced his or her own abuse as a child and, as a result, carries a sense of responsibility for his or her own pain. In contrast, you might feel angry that your abuser still has control over your life and, as a result, feel plagued by resentment.

Overwhelming feelings of hopelessness and despair: Many survivors of childhood trauma carry a deep existential loneliness or sense of despair. There can be an overpowering senselessness or lack of reason that accompanies trauma and abuse. As a result, you may have lost faith in people or in a higher power. These overwhelming feelings of hopelessness can interfere with your ability to find a sense of purpose or meaning in your life.

In addition to these core symptoms of C-PTSD, it is common to engage in other symptomatic behaviors to manage distressing emotions and memories. These behaviors can include skin picking, hair pulling, cutting, suicidal thoughts, eating disorders, impulsivity, and excessive risk-taking behaviors.

Common Misdiagnoses for C-PTSD

Historically, C-PTSD has not been well understood, even by mental health professionals. As a result, many people with childhood trauma have been misdiagnosed. Having the wrong diagnosis interferes with successful mental health care, especially if you have been prescribed the wrong medications or have experienced the wrong kind of treatment interventions. For example, difficulties with emotion regulation can lead you to feel anxious at certain times and depressed at other times. However, these "mood swings" might be misunderstood as symptoms of bipolar disorder if your treatment providers do not understand your trauma history.

Sometimes you might have more than one condition, and this may also lead to misdiagnosis. For example, you might have the co-occurring conditions of C-PTSD and attention deficit hyperactivity disorder (ADHD). Let's take a look at some of the common misdiagnoses or co-occurring diagnoses for C-PTSD:

- Borderline personality disorder or other personality disorders

- Bipolar disorder

- Attention deficit hyperactivity disorder (ADHD)

- Sensory processing disorder

- Learning disabilities

- Anxiety disorders, including panic and obsessive compulsive disorders

- Major depressive disorder or dysphoria

- Somatization disorders (experiencing psychological disorders as physical symptoms)

- Substance abuse or dependence

If, after reading this section, you believe that you have been misdiagnosed, discuss your concerns with a trusted therapist. Being informed about your own symptoms can help you feel empowered to advocate for your health-care needs.

MICHAEL

"I can't go on like this"

> "*Everything reminds me of how awful my life has been. I just know there is something wrong with me. I feel irritable and angry most of the time. Sometimes, I feel like I can't go on like this. What's the point of living?*"

Michael has suffered from unresolved childhood trauma for many years. His sense of desperation was worsening. As he and I got to know each other, I learned that Michael had experienced tremendous chaos in his childhood home. He grew up as a middle child with seven siblings. His mother was anxious and overwhelmed. His father was rarely home because he worked two jobs to pay the bills, but when he was around he would often become rageful. In therapy, Michael gained the tools to finally understand his own feelings of anger. As a child, he often felt lost in the chaos of his home. Now, with support, he was able to attend to his hurt and grief. In time, he realized that there was nothing wrong with him; his feelings were the result of growing up with parents who didn't meet his needs. While turning toward the pain of the past wasn't easy, it aided him in increasing his self-understanding and self-compassion, which has helped him feel hopeful for the first time in years.

Treating C-PTSD

This section will introduce you to the most common therapies for C-PTSD—namely, cognitive behavioral therapy (CBT), dialectical behavioral therapy (DBT), parts-work therapies, eye movement desensitization and reprocessing (EMDR) therapy, somatic psychology, and complementary and alternative medicine (CAM). Each has been well researched and shown to be effective.

Cognitive Behavioral Therapy (CBT)

Cognitive behavioral therapy (CBT) was developed by Dr. Aaron Beck as a way to help people struggling with anxiety or depression. Today, it is one of the most effective therapies for trauma recovery. CBT gives you the skills to examine the relationships between your thoughts, feelings, and behaviors and to identify patterns of thinking that worsen your emotional dysregulation. For example, trauma can leave you with an ongoing feeling of being unsafe. But if this feeling expands into a belief that you will never be safe, you might avoid leaving your house, which can lead to isolation and an increased sense of fear. This can result in a vicious cycle of loneliness that is self-reinforcing.

Several effective variations of CBT can help with trauma treatment. Acceptance and commitment therapy (ACT), developed by Dr. Steven Hayes, recognizes that difficult emotions are normal responses to painful life events. ACT invites you to turn toward these feelings with kindness and acceptance, which reduces your tendency to avoid unpleasant experiences.

Narrative exposure therapy (NET) was developed by Maggie Schauer, PhD; Thomas Elbert, PhD; and Frank Neuner. NET focuses on helping you process your emotions by guiding you to write a biographical narrative that includes both challenging moments and positive moments from your life. This life story helps you strengthen your sense of identity.

In general, CBT for trauma treatment employs a technique called "exposure," which involves reflecting upon or writing about your traumatic history. The aim of exposure is to reduce the distress you feel when thinking about painful events. Initially you might feel uncomfortable talking about the trauma, but with practice, exposure can help you develop a greater sense of control and more self-confidence.

For some with C-PTSD, exposure therapy can feel too direct. It is important to tell your therapist if any intervention doesn't feel right to you. Any therapy intervention should be something that you choose; it should never be a forced process.

Dialectical Behavioral Therapy (DBT)

Dialectical behavior therapy (DBT) was developed by Marsha Linehan, PhD, as a treatment for people with borderline personality disorder. DBT is a type of cognitive behavioral therapy that combines mindfulness and relaxation strategies. These skills are particularly helpful for the emotion dysregulation and interpersonal problems that are common in C-PTSD. DBT can help you learn to tolerate the distress of intense emotions without resorting to aggression, substance abuse, or other unhealthy coping mechanisms. DBT helps us understand that there is nothing inherently bad about having difficult emotions and that your thoughts and feelings don't define who you are. Mindfulness can help you cultivate a "compassionate witness"—the ability to nonjudgmentally and lovingly accept yourself.

DBT can also help you learn healthy ways to cope with the difficult feelings that can arise in relationships. For example, if you feel rejected by your partner, you might have the urge to yell. In this case, you would practice asking for closeness while refraining from making yourself or the other person wrong. This will help you build your self-respect. With practice, you can increase your capacity to handle conflicts with fairness and respect for yourself and for others.

Eye Movement Desensitization and Reprocessing (EMDR)

Eye movement desensitization and reprocessing (EMDR) therapy was developed by Dr. Francine Shapiro to relieve the distress associated with traumatic memories. The early phases of EMDR therapy help you develop positive resources to cope with this distress. For example, you might explore stress-reduction techniques or imagery that help you feel safe and relaxed. While the process of working through disturbing memories with EMDR is best achieved with a therapist, you can also practice it on your own.

Once you have sufficient coping strategies, EMDR helps you work through the distress of traumatic memories. This involves identifying the worst image related to the trauma, the associated negative belief, your emotions, and your bodily sensations. Then, EMDR invites you to attend to the distress of the traumatic memory by using "dual awareness," which asks you to simultaneously maintain conscious awareness of the experience of the here and now while focusing on the memory. EMDR then uses bilateral eye movements, which mimic REM sleep (the phase of sleep that allows you to process events and experiences from your life). The technique may also use tapping, listening to alternating tones through headphones, or holding small handheld devices that send vibrations between your left and right hands. Once you get to a point when you no longer feel disturbed while thinking about the memory, you are asked to focus on new, positive beliefs that will help you strengthen your sense of self.

Parts-Work Therapies

Childhood trauma can leave you feeling like you are at war with yourself. You might have a fierce inner critic, a strong need to be perfect, or a young part of you who feels small and powerless. Parts-work therapy recognizes that unresolved traumatic events from childhood can be held by parts of yourself until you have an opportunity to attend to your feelings and memories. There are several therapeutic approaches to working with these parts, notably, ego state interventions, developed by Robin Shapiro, and internal family systems therapy, created by Richard Schwartz.

Parts-work therapies are helpful especially if you have dissociative symptoms as part of C-PTSD. We tend to internalize our experiences of the family members whom we grew up with. For example, if you had a critical parent, this can become the voice of your own inner critic. Or, if you felt abandoned as a child, you might continue to neglect your own self-care needs now.

Parts work helps you to connect to your "adult" self. As an adult, you have a range of choices that weren't available to you as a child. Now, you can say no, assert your boundaries, ask for what you need, and protect yourself. As an adult, you can recognize that your painful feelings are connected to memories from your past—and that these events are over now. Once you are connected to your adult self, parts-work therapies focus on helping you compassionately attend to the vulnerable feelings and emotions held by the younger parts of your self.

Somatic Psychology

Somatic psychology focuses on body awareness within psychotherapy. Trauma takes a toll on our physiology and we experience many of the symptoms of C-PTSD within the body. For example, hypervigilance causes you to remain alert and unable to relax. This can get in the way of your ability to feel grounded or can lead to sleep problems because you are too vigilant to let your guard down. In contrast, depressive symptoms can leave you feeling sluggish, heavy, and tired.

Somatic therapies help you access the restorative and innate resilience of your body. The most common somatic therapies used today are Somatic Experiencing, developed by Peter Levine, and sensorimotor psychotherapy, developed by Pat Ogden. These therapies use sensory awareness, movement, and connection to breath as part of the healing process. Initially, somatic psychology helps build your resources by focusing on helping you feel grounded and aware of your bodily sensations. Then, you can work on the ways traumatic events remain stuck in your body.

Somatic psychology can help you heal from traumatic events even if you cannot remember exactly what happened. Rather than focusing on talking about your experiences, you concentrate on mindfully exploring your bodily sensations and emotions. For example, if you notice a tightness in your throat, you would allow movements or sounds that are related to this feeling. As you stay connected to your throat, you might recall a similar feeling from childhood. This process can then help you release long-held emotions, such as a longing for connection or grief about a loss. Through this therapy, you might discover a feeling of openness in your body or a sense that you have "found your voice." Ultimately, somatic psychology can help you integrate and embody new positive states of self-assuredness or empowerment.

Complementary and Alternative Medicine (CAM)

Childhood trauma can cause health challenges in adulthood, including digestive problems, fibromyalgia, and autoimmune and chronic pain conditions. Like somatic psychology, complementary and alternative medicine (CAM) focuses on the mind–body connection, this time with an emphasis on nutrition, massage therapy, relaxation strategies, exercise, meditation, and yoga.

Unresolved traumatic stress contributes to imbalances in the autonomic nervous system—the system that controls subconscious functions in our bodies, like our heartbeat. The autonomic nervous system is divided into two subsystems—the sympathetic nervous system and the parasympathetic nervous system—which regulate the finer points of our bodily processes, like blood pressure and pupil dilation. The sympathetic nervous system takes over when we feel threatened, getting us ready to fight, flee, or freeze. The parasympathetic nervous system comes in when the threat is gone and it helps us get back to a place of calm. If you have faced repeated stress, you might notice a tendency to remain in a state of high alert, without being able to rest, or you might feel stuck in a low-arousal state of fatigue, leaving you feeling foggy or dizzy. You might relate to both these patterns, in which case you alternate between feeling overwhelmed and shutting down. Mind–body therapies can help balance your autonomic nervous system.

Healing in Stages

Healing from C-PTSD ideally happens in stages. The first of these stages establishes safety and stabilization. For example, using the healing strategies in this book, you can build your capacity to be mindful of the present moment by sensing and feeling your body. This phase of treatment focuses on building your resources by recalling the times you have felt safe, connected to another person, or compassionate toward yourself. These tools will help you differentiate the present from the past.

The second stage involves facing and working through traumatic memories using CBT, EMDR therapy, and somatic psychology. You might not feel ready to move toward trauma resolution and integration. In this case, you can focus on using the healing strategies provided in this book for safety and stabilization for as long as you need. Once you feel ready, you can carefully pace yourself by attending to small bits of traumatic memories while regularly engaging with your resources to keep you feeling safe and grounded. This will aid in ensuring that you do not become flooded or overwhelmed when thinking about the past.

Turning toward the traumatic events of the past naturally evolves into the third stage of healing, which involves integrating the parts of yourself that have had to remain separate for the sake of survival. Often, this stage involves reflecting upon your relationship to meaning and purpose. This involves acknowledging the ways that you have grown as a result of the painful events of your past.

What About Medication?

Many people with C-PTSD turn to doctors and psychiatrists for help. Sometimes, well-meaning physicians prescribe medications as a stand-alone treatment, without also making a referral for psychotherapy. While medications can be helpful to reduce your symptoms, trauma experts recommend using them alongside therapy. It is also important to understand the various types of medications so that you can make an informed decision about their place in your healing process. Let's take a closer look:

SSRIs: Selective serotonin reuptake inhibitors (SSRIs) such as Prozac, Zoloft, or Paxil are usually used as antidepressants, but can also be used for trauma. They are most effective for decreasing hyper-arousal and mood symptoms, including anger, irritability, and depression. However, they are less effective in managing re-experiencing or dissociative symptoms.

Benzodiazepines: Benzodiazepines such as Valium, Xanax, Ativan, and Klonopin are typically prescribed because of their fast-acting reduction of anxiety, sleep disturbance, and physical pain. In 2012, this class of medications was reclassified as harmful for PTSD because they are highly addictive and prolong the healing process. They have actually been shown to worsen anxiety, increase irritability, and increase sleep disturbances when used over time. They also exacerbate suppression of the autonomic nervous system, increasing your risk of dissociative symptoms.

Prescription stimulants: Medications for ADHD such as Adderall and Ritalin can be helpful when you need to focus, but these stimulants can be harmful if you have experienced a recent trauma. They cause the direct release of norepinephrine in the brain, which helps in the formation of vivid, long-lasting memories and can increase feelings of anxiety.

New and experimental treatments: Additional medications are showing promising results for the treatment of trauma. These include prazosin, ketamine, and low-dose naltrexone. Prazosin helps to reduce nightmares. Ketamine helps to reduce depressive symptoms and suicidal ideation. Low-dose naltrexone is especially helpful for dissociative symptoms and chronic-pain conditions.

How Am I Doing?

As you come to the end of this chapter, I invite you to take a moment to pause and reflect. Do you relate to the description of C-PTSD and similar symptoms described here? Have you been misdiagnosed or felt that your health care was poorly managed? If so, it is important to discuss this information with your therapist. This will help you work together to arrive at an accurate diagnosis and develop an appropriate treatment plan. In addition, notice if anything you've read so far has left you feeling activated or triggered. If so, this is a time to focus on self-care. There are many resources offered throughout this book, starting with the first healing strategy, "Reclaim Choice." Remember, you can immediately start using any of these coping strategies at any time.

Healing Strategy:
Reclaim Choice

The symptoms of C-PTSD can leave you feeling flooded with emotion and overwhelmed. It is easy to lose a sense of choice about whether or when to think about the trauma. A valuable healing strategy is to reclaim choice and control. In this practice, you give yourself the option to put away or contain disturbing thoughts, feelings, emotions, and memories. Often, this requires that you make an agreement with yourself to consciously set aside the time to heal your childhood trauma. For example, you do not want to think about traumatic memories when you are at work or while parenting a child. However, an appointment with a therapist is a supportive place and time when you can address the trauma of your past and begin to heal.

Take some time to explore the following two approaches to the healing strategy "Reclaim Choice":

- Make a verbal agreement with yourself that you will attend to your traumatic memories at the right time and in the right space, such as with your therapist. Mentally, give yourself permission to not think about your traumatic past right now. Take several deep breaths, reminding yourself that you have the choice as to whether or when to think about any distressing memories from your past.
- If you notice that disturbing feelings, images, emotions, or sensations continue to intrude, give yourself permission to write about your distress. Set a timer for 10 to 15 minutes and write down what comes to mind. When the timer goes off, it is time to close your journal. Know that these upsetting memories can be held safely inside your journal until you return to therapy.

All new behaviors become easier with practice. You can return to this healing strategy as often as needed, until you feel that you have more of a sense of choice about whether or when to think about the trauma.

2

Healing Avoidance Symptoms

"I Am Learning to Be Here Now"

Have you ever withdrawn from social situations, eaten food to numb yourself from emotional pain, or had too much to drink after you felt triggered by a reminder of your past? If so, you are not alone. These are examples of avoidance behaviors, and they are common symptoms among survivors of childhood trauma. In this chapter, we will explore why you might have an urge to push away people or places that remind you of the past. The strategies in this chapter will help you learn to mindfully increase your sense of safety here and now and to replace avoidance with wiser coping behaviors. This will help you live a more fulfilling life and aid in improving your relationships with others.

ALICIA

"I think about running away"

Alicia walked into my office and sat on the edge of the chair closest to the door. She explained that she felt jumpy and jittery in her body. In her words, "I think about running away almost all of the time." The first agreement we had established in therapy was that she had permission to leave, and I reminded her of this. Immediately I noticed a subtle settling in as she sat a little farther back in her chair.

When we started to look at Alicia's urge to run, she shared with me a memory of her father's berating her for every little thing. She said, "I would have to stand there while he said horrible things to me." She then shared that, as a teenager, she had promised herself that she would never let herself get stuck in an abusive situation again. She has been running away ever since. The painful part was that now Alicia was running away from people and places that were safe, loving, and kind.

Alicia and I talked about how we develop coping strategies as children to help us survive these kinds of repeated frightening events and that these same coping mechanisms can backfire as we become adults. With practice, she was able to develop new, more effective strategies to help her feel safe. She learned to differentiate the past from the present so that she could benefit from new, positive opportunities in her life. In one of our last sessions, she said, "I am learning to be here now."

Understanding Avoidance

Avoidance symptoms are the behaviors that distance you from painful images, thoughts, emotions, or sensations related to traumatic memories. Some common avoidance behaviors include staying away from people or places that evoke painful memories, isolating yourself, emotional eating, and substance use. You may rely heavily on thinking as a way to avoid feeling emotions. Or, like Alicia, you might continue to avoid people or places even though they are safe.

As you learned in chapter 1, childhood trauma happened during a time when you were young and dependent upon your caregivers. Sometimes, we cope by becoming the "good child" who develops competence or perfectionism to deal with the chaos of home. Some children create an idealized fantasy that their parents were actually safe and good when, in reality, they weren't.

Dissociation

In most cases, children are not able to fight or run away from abusive parents. Or if they try, they may make a bad situation worse. There may be no protection or support from caring adults. If you experienced these types of situations, you may have developed dissociative symptoms as a way to avoid the pain. This can leave you feeling dizzy, foggy, or disconnected from your body. Or, you might have created distinctly different parts of yourself—parts that hold your distress and pain in order to survive. Depending upon the severity of dissociative symptoms, you might feel like your world is surreal, or you might arrive at places with no memory of how you got there.

The coping mechanisms we develop in childhood tend to backfire when they continue into adulthood. For example, a pattern of perfectionism often leads to high levels of self-criticism or an intolerance of other people's mistakes. Or, if you rely upon an idealized version of your childhood, you might deny the impact of your parents' harsh or critical treatment of you. You might say, "They were being tough with me for my own good," or "Yeah, my dad hit me, but it was no big deal." You might distance yourself from your emotional pain by relying too heavily on thinking, analyzing, or keeping busy.

Flashbacks

You might notice a strong urge to avoid your feelings after a triggering event such as a conflict with a loved one or a movie that reminds you of your childhood. Triggering events can cause invasive symptoms such as flashbacks (we will discuss these at length in chapter 3). One way to think of avoidance is that it is similar to having a phobia, but instead of having a phobia of heights or spiders, you feel phobic of your own emotions or bodily sensations. For example, a certain smell might remind you of your childhood home. Suddenly, you feel flooded with an intolerable feeling of discomfort. As a result, you behave in a way that makes that feeling go away. You might drink too much, immerse yourself in a work project, or exercise excessively. Unfortunately, these coping mechanisms can leave you feeling cut off from yourself or from your loved ones.

One of the ways you can heal is to explore your history and ask yourself why you needed to push away your pain. You might recall times that you decided it was not safe to be vulnerable. Remember that avoidance behaviors may have been the best way for you to survive at a time when you didn't have the support or resources you needed. This awareness can help you increase your self-compassion.

Start Healing Yourself

In order to heal, it is important to realize that you are no longer living in the unsafe environment of your childhood. You are an adult now and can make new choices, which include learning new and healthier coping strategies. This chapter will offer mindfulness techniques to help you recognize that you are safe now. You will be invited to compassionately increase your self-awareness of your own avoidance behaviors. The third strategy will help you develop healthy distractions so that you can replace harmful behaviors with healthier choices. In this section, you will read about Xavier, Lisa, and Rachel and the ways that avoidance symptoms were disrupting their lives. Moreover, you will learn three practical, research-based strategies to start healing from your own avoidance symptoms.

XAVIER

"I didn't leave the house for three days"

"About a year ago, my girlfriend broke up with me. That afternoon, I had a panic attack, and when I came home I fell asleep on my couch. I didn't leave the house for three days. This scared me. That's why I came to therapy. Until now, I've never told anyone about how my parents would scream at each other, especially when my dad was drunk. I would go into my room and hide under my bed, all alone. Now, when I feel stressed I hide in my house, just like I did when I was a kid."

Sometimes, the traumatic events of the past can feel as though they are still happening today. Through our work together, Xavier learned to mindfully engage his senses so that he could feel safe, here and now. Like Xavier, you might feel as if you are still reliving an experience that ended many years ago. In order to heal, it is important to recognize that the events of your childhood are over.

Healing Strategy:
Mindfulness of the Here and Now

This healing strategy involves mentally acknowledging that you are safe. However, it is important to ensure that you are, indeed, safe. If you are currently living in a threatening environment, you need to realize that the feeling of fear is essential for your self-protection, and the first thing to focus on is getting safe. But if you are suffering from anxiety related to the past and you are in a safe situation, you can use this strategy to engage your senses so that you can let go of unnecessary fear. You do not need to practice all of these steps or do them in any specific order. Experiment and discover what works best for you.

- Take a look around you and notice details in your space. Are there any visual cues that can serve as reminders that you are safe now? Is there any item, such as a plant or piece of artwork, that you find pleasant? Notice how it feels to move your head and eyes as you look around your space.

- Say to yourself soothing words, such as "I am safe now" or "I am okay." Speak these words out loud in a gentle and loving tone. Notice how it feels to hear your voice speaking with kindness.
- Bring one hand over the opposite arm. Notice how it feels to gently and lovingly touch your arm with your hand. Notice the feel of your skin under your palm. Notice the warmth of your palm against your arm. Repeat this practice on the opposite arm.
- Take a sip of water or warm tea and move your tongue around the inside of your mouth. Sense the back of your teeth or the roof of your mouth with your tongue. Notice the taste or temperature.
- Take several deep breaths while focusing on the rise and fall of your belly. Notice the sensation in your body, or perhaps just focus on the feel of air moving across the tip of your nose.

There are many additional ways to use your senses to increase your mindfulness of the here and now. For example, you might listen to a soothing piece of music or you could hold a rock in your hand, noticing its texture or temperature. You can get creative with this process. Most importantly, if any sensory experience is upsetting to you, you can switch to another sensory exploration until you experience a feeling of ease in body and mind.

LISA

"I spend my life taking care of everyone else, ignoring myself"

"Life was chaotic when I was growing up. After my parents' divorce, I moved back and forth between them, but I was always in the middle. My mom was depressed and my dad was angry. There was no place for me. I became really good at not having needs and feelings. Now, instead of asking people for help, I spend my life taking care of everyone else."

Lisa learned to push away her own needs and take care of others as a means of coping with her chaotic childhood. Sometimes we engage in avoidance behaviors automatically, out of habit. By taking the time to build self-awareness of avoidance behaviors, we can create change. In Lisa's case, she was able to recognize that she was protecting herself from the pain she felt as a child. Furthermore, she was able to identify current situations that led her to ignore her needs. For example, she realized she was avoiding the possibility of rejection by not asking for help when she needed it. Therapy helped her to be more vulnerable and to take risks, even if this meant she might be disappointed. Ultimately, she felt rewarded for her efforts.

Healing Strategy: Self-Awareness of Avoidance Behaviors

This healing strategy involves taking a compassionate yet honest look at your own avoidance symptoms. Take a few breaths and set an intention to mindfully observe your experiences with a capacity to lovingly accept yourself, just as you are. One of the most important components of mindfulness is an attitude of nonjudgment and curiosity about your experience. Mindfulness practices remind us that self-acceptance is vital for change. Take a look at the list that follows and notice if any of these common behaviors are relevant to you and your life:

- I stay away from people or places.
- I isolate myself.
- I tend to overeat when I feel emotional.
- I drink too much or use substances to avoid my pain.
- I spend hours playing video games or watching TV.
- I don't want to admit to myself that I was abused or neglected.
- I spend so much time caring for others that I ignore myself.
- I want to control myself or others.
- I am a perfectionist.
- I cancel or forget to go to therapy appointments.
- I bury myself in my work so I don't have to feel.
- I rely heavily on thinking so as to avoid feeling.
- I sometimes numb out or dissociate.

Once you have identified your avoidance behaviors, take a few minutes to reflect on how these behaviors started. For example, you might remember developing tendencies toward perfectionism or self-control so as to manage the chaos of your childhood home, or you might recall the first time you drank alcohol to numb your pain. Now, take a few minutes to reflect upon current situations that make you want to engage in your avoidance behaviors. What current events trigger you to push away your pain or avoid your feelings?

RACHEL

"I can't stop myself from eating"

"I wake up early, go to the gym, and am good at my work. I even go out after work for happy hour. But when I get home at the end of the day, I feel so lonely. Then, I can't stop myself from eating until I feel sick. It's the only way I know how to numb the pain, but I always wake up feeling worse the next day."

Rachel's story is a reminder that many people with C-PTSD use food, alcohol, or drugs to push away distressing emotions or memories associated with childhood trauma. In Rachel's case, she relied upon emotional eating to avoid having to face the loneliness that comprised much of her childhood. Once Rachel identified that she was avoiding her pain through eating, she was able to learn to cope with that feeling in a healthier manner. She was relieved to have a new set of behaviors that didn't leave her feeling so bad about herself.

Healing Strategy:
Develop Healthy Distractions

Drawn from dialectical behavioral therapy (DBT), this healing strategy explores healthy ways to distract yourself from distressing emotions or memories. Create a list of positive coping behaviors that you can use to replace existing avoidance behaviors, especially if those existing behaviors have harmful consequences. You might discover that you can still use some of your existing avoidance strategies for coping, so long as you use them in moderation.

This healing strategy is not about working through the pain of your traumatic past. That is for another time. Instead, distraction is a short-term solution that can help you prevent a behavior you might later regret. Take some time to look over the following list of positive coping behaviors or create your own. You can return to this list anytime you feel an urge to cope with your pain in a harmful way.

- Spend time in nature or go for a walk in your neighborhood.
- Go to a favorite coffee shop.
- Watch a movie that evokes a new emotion (such as a comedy, if you are feeling angry).
- Play a video game for a short while.
- Read an uplifting or inspiring book.
- Move your body in a healthy way (stretch, yoga, exercise without overdoing it).
- Listen to a favorite piece of music.
- Draw or use a coloring book.
- Smell the scent of an essential oil you find soothing.
- Do simple tasks around the house (vacuuming, laundry, dishes).

- Count five things that you are grateful for.
- Remind yourself that this pain is temporary and that it will pass.

How Am I Doing?

This chapter focused on helping you identify how you avoid distressing C-PTSD symptoms. I invite you take a moment to pause and reflect. How did you feel reading the stories of others who experienced childhood trauma? Did anything in this chapter leave you feeling unsettled? Were you able to find relief using any of the healing strategies? Remember, you can pace yourself by pausing at regular intervals to practice self-care or by reaching out to a loved one or therapist for extra support. We'll end this chapter with one more healing strategy to add to your self-care toolbox.

Healing Strategy:
Peaceful Place Visualization

Creative visualization can be helpful in healing C-PTSD. The brain doesn't differentiate between real or imagined experiences, so focusing your mind on positive visualization can be a powerful tool.

For this next practice, take your time thinking of a place that feels peaceful and calm. This might be an actual place or it can be an imagined place—maybe a place in nature, such as the seashore or a mountaintop. Or, you might choose a building that is a healing sanctuary. Once you have identified a peaceful place, use your senses to heighten the image. Take a look around your imagined space. What do you see? What do you hear? How do you feel in your body? Would you like to have anyone with you in your peaceful place? To ensure that your space feels calm and peaceful, are there any safeguards you need to put into place, such as a tall fence or a door with a lock? You are in charge of who gets to come into your peaceful place.

Once you have developed your peaceful place, take a few deep breaths and notice how you feel in your body and mind. Remember, you can return to this place as often as you choose.

3

Healing Invasive and Intrusive Symptoms

"I Am Finally Able to Feel Safe"

If you are reading this book as a survivor of childhood trauma, then it is likely you have experienced hypervigilance, feelings of panic, nightmares, or a general sense of anxiety. You may have felt or continue to feel triggered by certain events. You might have flashbacks in which you experience a rush of images, emotions, or bodily sensations connected to the trauma. These kinds of re-experiencing symptoms often disrupt the lives of trauma survivors and can last for hours or even days. In this chapter, we will explore these invasive and intrusive symptoms and, more importantly, present coping strategies that can help you feel grounded.

SIERRA

"It is so hard for me to relax"

"I have a difficult time going to sleep at night. That is when I feel overwhelmed by all of the scary feelings. I get easily startled by sounds and then my heart starts to race. It is so hard for me to relax."

Sierra was exhausted. She had been having a difficult time sleeping for several months after she had been in a car accident. Even though she took sleep medication, her anxious feelings kept coming back. As I got to know Sierra, I learned that she had always identified as a "tough girl," someone who could handle anything. She told me that when she was little, her mother would rage and scream at her. She learned to hide her fear and pretend that she didn't care. But ever since the car accident, she felt shaken and fragile. When we began to explore the feeling of being scared, Sierra shared that it reminded her of how she had felt as a young girl. This accident brought those feelings to the surface.

Initially, therapy helped Sierra recognize that she was having flashbacks, a common symptom of C-PTSD. We helped her strengthen her resources so she could remind herself that she was safe now, even though she was having scary feelings. She learned breathing and relaxation techniques to help with her sleep. Then, we focused on building self-compassion for the vulnerable feelings that were held inside the "tough girl" for so many years. As a result of these practices, she was relieved to share: "I am finally able to feel safe; now I can settle my anxiety."

Understanding Invasive and Intrusive Symptoms

Sierra's story represents a common experience among C-PTSD survivors: invasive and intrusive symptoms that arise after a recent traumatic event. Sometimes the recent event is as extreme as a car accident; other times, the triggering event can be more subtle. For example, an expression on someone's face or a certain tone of voice might bring fear, anger, or a feeling of rejection. The triggering event can lead to a flashback—a resurgence of images, emotions, or bodily sensations related to a traumatic event from the past in which you feel as if that event is happening now. Like Sierra's experience, these symptoms can flood you with anxiety, making it difficult to relax or sleep.

Those re-experiencing symptoms are often associated with high-arousal states such as anxiety, panic, and hypervigilance. *Invasive* refers to the way these symptoms invade your consciousness, and *intrusive* refers to the way these symptoms intrude upon your ability to feel safe and relaxed. You may experience the distress physically: a rapid heart rate, tightness in your chest, difficulty breathing, or challenges with your digestion. Anxiety can lead you to become highly sensitive to other people's body language, facial expressions, and voice tone. All these symptoms are related to the sympathetic nervous system, which prepares you to fight or flee a dangerous situation.

Hijacking the Brain

Flashbacks can also be connected to low-arousal feelings in which you feel ashamed, small, powerless, or helpless (we will discuss these low-arousal symptoms in greater depth in chapters 4 and 8). In some cases, flashbacks are connected to memories that happened when you were too young to form images or verbal memories, or your brain may be trying to protect you from traumatic memories with dissociative symptoms. In these cases, you might feel flooded by emotions or sensations with no known cause, but you might be acutely aware that you are having a flashback. We will discuss dissociative symptoms in chapter 6.

Unfortunately, people with complex PTSD have a difficult time feeling safe, even in situations where there is no current threat. This is because it can be difficult to differentiate between experiences that occurred in the past and what is happening now. You might believe that people or places are dangerous, when you are actually safe. It is also common to scan your environment and the faces of people around you for any signs of threat. This can become a negativity bias that leads you to ignore signs of safety.

Invasive symptoms evoke emotions and body states that are neurobiologically connected to memories of other times when you felt the same way. This is called "state-dependent memory" and it explains why, when you feel sad, you are more likely to remember other times that you were sad. Memories are stored in the brain, interconnected with other similar memories. Therefore, when you feel triggered into a state of panic, you are more likely to go down a rabbit hole full of interconnected traumatic memories related to times when you felt frightened.

Dr. Daniel Goleman, author of the book *Emotional Intelligence*, explains that flashbacks cause the brain to become emotionally hijacked by strong emotions such as fear or anger. When we feel safe, we are able to rely upon the most recently evolved part of the brain, called the prefrontal cortex. This part of the brain helps us to reflect upon our actions and make wise decisions based on our goals for the future.

However, when threatened, the midbrain and lower brain center become activated and they reduce blood flow to the prefrontal cortex. The midbrain, also called the limbic system, is highly sensitized to danger. The lower brain, also called the reptilian brain, activates our most primitive, self-protective defenses. In short, when we experience an actual or perceived threat, we tend to react defensively, without thinking about the consequences.

Intrusive Memories

Intrusive symptoms can arise as a result of a wide range of triggers—events or situations that can bring back memories of trauma. A trigger can be anything that causes you to remember uncomfortable feelings from the past, such as making a phone call to a family member, returning to your childhood home, watching a scene in a movie, reading an article in the news, or smelling a certain soap, perfume, or cologne that was worn by an abuser. Other common triggers might be experiencing a conflict with a partner or child or making a common mistake, such as forgetting someone's name or getting a parking ticket. Instead of being able to brush off this normal, human misstep you might feel excessively critical and punitive toward yourself.

When we experience a threat, whether it is real or perceived, our breathing changes, usually subconsciously. Your breathing might be more shallow or rapid when you see a person who has hurt you, for example. This happens because our bodies want to prepare us to fight or flee. Our bodies think we are being threatened. Animals experience this response, too, but once safe, an animal will release the stress by shaking, moving, or breathing deeply. However, we humans often stay in high-arousal states long after the "threat" has passed. This is because we have highly developed brains that have evolved to process our experiences with language and thought. In addition, many of us have been taught that sitting still is a sign of polite obedience, so we have learned to suppress our instinctual connection to sensation and movement.

One way to restore balance to the body and mind is to focus on rebalancing the autonomic nervous system. We can do this by stimulating the vagus nerve, which can be thought of as a bi-directional information highway that communicates perceptions of safety or threat between your brain and body. This stimulation can help us access the restorative and healing qualities of the parasympathetic nervous system. One of the fastest ways to balance your nervous system is with the breath, as you will explore in the first healing strategy of the next section.

Start Healing Yourself

In this section, you will read about Tamara and Ben, and their experiences of invasive and intrusive symptoms. You will learn the strategies that helped them heal from C-PTSD. The three research-based strategies in this chapter come from yoga therapy, cognitive behavioral therapy, and acceptance and commitment therapy. Using these tools, you will be better able to identify when you are having re-experiencing symptoms and, as a result, will reduce the time it takes to find balance.

TAMARA

"I still get a stomachache when I think about it"

"My mother never hit me—she didn't have to. All she had to do was look at me in that critical, disapproving way and I cowered. Every day of my childhood was like this. I was never enough to be accepted or loved. I always felt like I was in trouble and about to get punished. I still get a stomachache when I think about it."

Tamara's story is painfully common—a harsh and judgmental look on a parent's face has lasting consequences. One of the physical consequences is Tamara's stomachache. Other common physical experiences include sweating profusely, having difficulty relaxing or sleeping, feeling a tightness in your chest, having a rapid heart rate, and experiencing difficulty breathing. These serve as reminders that often we cannot simply think our way out of flashbacks.

Healing Strategy:
Restorative Breath

Every time you breathe in, you engage your sympathetic nervous system, while each exhale engages your parasympathetic system. You can turn on your body's relaxation response by exhaling longer than you inhale.

To experiment, explore inhaling to a count of 4 and exhaling to a count of 8, while silently counting in your head. Continue for about 10 breaths, and then notice how you feel. If you would like to experiment with a variation on this relaxation breath, you can explore a 4-7-8 breath by holding your breath for a count of 7 between your inhalation and exhalation. If at any point you notice that holding your breath creates a feeling of anxiety or panic, reduce the length of time you hold your breath or drop the hold all together. Most importantly, this is an experiment. It is wise to take your time and notice the feedback you receive from your body and mind. Remember, the healing strategies in this book are not one-size-fits-all. Rather, you can fine-tune and adapt these practices until you find reliable strategies that work for you.

BEN

"I lost my temper, but I can't explain why"

"The other night, I was sitting at the dinner table with my wife and teenage sons. Our lives are stressful; I have my work, my wife runs a business, and our sons have school and their sports. That night, like most nights, the boys were hungry and my wife wanted to share about her day. Suddenly, I felt like no one was listening to me. I became so angry that I had to leave the table and lock myself in my room to stop myself from screaming at everyone. I lost my temper, but I can't explain why."

Ben's story teaches us that sometimes flashbacks happen even if we don't understand why they have been triggered. His reaction to his wife and kids came out of what seemed like nowhere, but he was able to recognize that his reaction was disproportionate to their behaviors. Though he wasn't able to stop himself from feeling hurt and angry, he was self-aware enough to leave the table before he erupted. In therapy, he was able to explore the feeling of not being heard, which he later identified as a wound from his childhood. Once Ben understood the triggering event, he was able to have greater self-compassion for his feelings, which allowed him to talk calmly to his wife and sons about his needs.

Healing Strategy:
Self-Awareness of Triggers

Developing self-awareness of triggers is one of the most important strategies for managing invasive and intrusive symptoms. If you know you are getting triggered into a flashback, you are more likely to immediately use your strategies to calm yourself down and feel safe. Self-awareness of triggers can also help you predict when you might face potentially upsetting events, which will allow you to prepare.

The first step in this healing practice is to become aware of your triggers. Take some time to review the list that follows and write down any triggers that are relevant to you. Common triggers include the following:

- Contact with historically abusive family members (phone calls, visits)
- Returning to your childhood home
- Recent events that remind you of your childhood trauma (e.g., a scene in a movie, an article in the news, etc.)
- Experiencing conflict with a loved one (spouse, partner, child, friend)
- Feeling alone, abandoned, or rejected
- Feeling out of control
- Experiencing a sensory reminder of the past, such as a smell, sound, or taste
- Making mistakes (e.g., getting a parking ticket, dropping and breaking a dish)

Once you have identified your triggering events, take a few minutes to reflect upon the emotions that arise in you with each triggering event. Do you feel afraid, angry, sad, or helpless? Or do you become excessively self-critical? Notice the feeling that you have in your body with each triggering event. Do you feel anxious or jumpy? Is your heart racing? In contrast, do you feel frozen, like you can't move? Or do you feel collapsed and fatigued? See if you can explore these experiences with self-compassion. Lastly, take a moment to consider whether these emotions and sensations feel familiar. Do you recall times in your childhood when you had similar feelings? These memories may serve as clues to the unfinished business of your childhood.

Once you have gained self-awareness of triggering events, you might choose to share this information with your therapist or with loved ones so they can help to compassionately support you. In some cases, awareness of re-experiencing symptoms can help you make wise decisions to stay away from triggering situations. Most importantly, even though invasive and intrusive symptoms are uncomfortable, they can also help you identify issues to discuss in therapy so that this pain can provide an opportunity for healing.

How Am I Doing?

This chapter focused on helping you identify invasive and intrusive symptoms of C-PTSD. I invite you take a moment to reflect. Could you relate to the stories that were shared? Has any part of this chapter left you feeling distressed? Have any of the healing strategies helped you feel more confident in your ability to handle challenging memories? If so, I encourage you to return to those practices as needed. We'll end this chapter with one more healing strategy that comes from acceptance and commitment therapy (ACT) to add to your self-care toolbox.

Healing Strategy:
The Weather Report and Forecast

Emotions are like the weather. This practice invites you to take a mindful look at your current weather report. For example, you might notice that you feel calm and relaxed like a sunny day. Or, maybe you feel stirred up like a tornado because someone ignored your boundaries.

You can create a "weather forecast" as you prepare for upcoming events. Just as a prediction of rain helps you remember to bring your umbrella, you are better able to prepare yourself when you take an honest look at challenging events. For example, if you know you are visiting with a critical family member, you might plan for stormy emotions of sadness, hurt, and anger. This awareness can remind you to make changes so you can feel more protected, grounded, and connected to your center, such as staying at a hotel instead of in your childhood home. Or, you might choose not to visit at all.

Take a few breaths, then create a weather report for your current emotional landscape. Reflect upon any events that may have shaped this weather pattern. Now that you have gained awareness of your emotions, see if you can offer yourself the gift of self-acceptance. For example, you might say to yourself, "I am okay just as I am" or "My emotions are welcome here."

Now, think about an upcoming event. Can you create a weather forecast that predicts how you might feel? You can prepare for the muddy, messy moments of life by paying attention to the signs of a storm ahead. Remember, though, that we cannot always predict the weather accurately. Sometimes, how you actually feel in the moment may be different from what you expected. As you practice your weather forecasts, notice if your accuracy increases over time.

4

Healing Depressive Symptoms

"I Feel Connected to Myself Again"

Childhood trauma can leave you feeling powerless or help-less, especially if there was no way to stop the abuse or get the love you needed. When trauma is ongoing, these feelings of helplessness can form the basis of your sense of self. In this chapter, you will gain an understanding of depressive symp-toms in the context of C-PTSD. You will learn the healing strategies that help you combat negative thinking, embrace your emotions, and connect to a feeling of empowerment in your body. While depressive symptoms are the result of your past, they do not need to define your future.

BRYAN

"No matter what I did, nothing made a difference"

"My parents divorced when I was 8 years old. Afterwards, my mother fell apart and went away for a year. I lived with my father and older brother. That same year, my brother began to beat me up after school. I tried to talk to my dad, but he told me to stop being a crybaby. I felt helpless. No matter what I did, nothing made a difference."

Bryan's story is an example of the powerlessness a child feels when facing persistent trauma without the protection of a caring adult. As an adult, Bryan suffered from symptoms of depression. He struggled with negative thoughts about his future, had difficulty concentrating, and lost his enthusiasm for life. His primary-care doctor prescribed him antidepressants, but he was also wise enough to ask Bryan about his childhood history. Once he learned that Bryan had faced neglect and abuse, he made a referral for therapy.

Therapy helped Bryan recognize that his history of unresolved childhood trauma was contributing to his depression. Initially, he practiced CBT and used mindfulness tools to reduce his patterns of negative thinking and to tame his fierce inner critic. Then, we focused on helping him compassionately work with the painful emotions from his childhood. While it was difficult to turn toward the pain, this process helped him feel fully alive after being numb and shut down for many years. Bryan cried tears of relief as he told me: "I feel connected to myself again."

Understanding Depression from Trauma

Depressive symptoms include irritability, a loss of interest or pleasure in things that you previously enjoyed, or feeling hopeless about your future. You might find yourself ruminating on worst-case scenarios or you might notice changes in your eating and sleeping habits. It is not uncommon for treatment providers to focus on a diagnosis of depression without recognizing that these symptoms can be a result of complex trauma. C-PTSD and depression have symptoms that overlap, and just as we saw in Bryan's story, sometimes it is possible to have both. The healing strategies in this chapter will help you cope with your depressive symptoms, regardless of the cause.

As a result of childhood trauma, you may have felt that no one could handle your feelings or that no one would respond to you in a loving and supportive way. You may have learned to push away feelings of rejection, hurt, or anger. Now, as an adult, you might continue to distance yourself from your feelings or deny your needs. But these emotions may still build up inside of you: You might feel irritable or you might blow up in explosive anger and hurt or scare others. Feelings of shame and embarrassment may then fuel your inner critic and initiate a vicious cycle that reinforces the urge to further push away your emotions.

Dr. Stephen Porges, professor of psychiatry and author of *The Polyvagal Theory*, teaches us that the parasympathetic nervous system shows up in two ways, depending upon whether we feel safe or threatened. When we feel safe, the parasympathetic nervous system brings about rest and relaxation. However, when we feel threatened, the parasympathetic nervous system can go into a defensive mode associated with trauma, known as a "faint response," which includes feelings of helplessness, fatigue, and eventual collapse. When a child spends an extended period of time in a faint response, these feelings of heaviness, sluggishness, and tiredness persist into adulthood and can influence their overall sense of self.

Psychologically, when there is no way to escape repeated emotional or physical abuse, we feel powerless. Even if you are no longer living in a traumatizing environment, you might still feel helpless. You may have a wide range of choices and behaviors available to you now, but it can be difficult to see or engage in these new positive and life-affirming possibilities. Psychologist and researcher Dr. Martin Seligman describes this "learned helplessness" as pervasive feelings of powerlessness accompanied by beliefs that nothing can or will ever change.

Cognitive behavioral therapy (CBT) sees depression as a triad of thinking patterns: a negative view of yourself, a negative view of the world, and a negative view of the future. For example, you might feel you are incompetent and there is no point in trying to heal because the world has and will continue to repeatedly fail you. As hard as this may sound, it is essential that you challenge self-limiting beliefs in order to heal from depressive symptoms.

Depression is often caused by anger that has been turned inward as self-hatred. Healing involves reclaiming your ability to accept and express your emotions. Feeling angry about times you were mistreated can help you become empowered to protect yourself. As you explore the healing strategies in this chapter, you will learn to work with your mind, emotions, and body to feel empowered in your life now.

Start Healing Yourself

In this section, we will explore some of the common experiences of depression as described by Jenna and Leo. The first healing strategy will help you awaken your compassionate witness so that you can become a mindful observer of your thoughts. This will help you recognize the voice of your inner critic. With this awareness, you can learn to protect yourself by standing up for your underlying needs and feelings.

The burden of unexpressed emotions can leave you feeling heavy and weighted down, as if you have been carrying a heavy backpack for many years. The second healing strategy encourages you to feel your emotions and empty the backpack. Releasing the weight of painful emotions can allow you to feel lighter and freer. As a result, you might notice that you no longer want to stay curled up on your couch. Your desire to move, stretch, and engage in life can become easier to realize.

The final healing strategy of this chapter will help you incorporate physical movement and exercise into your life so you can find relief from the physiological effects of depression.

JENNA

"I just can't do anything right"

▼

"Everyone else seems to have it together, but I always seem to say the wrong thing at the wrong time. I just can't do anything right! What is wrong with me?"

Jenna sat on the couch with her shoulders hunched over and her head hung forward. She was under attack from a vicious inner critic. Her negative self-talk was fueled by over-generalizations and unfair comparisons about how she imagined others to be. Her mind was obsessively looping with beliefs that she could never do things right. As a result, she was feeling a looming sense of despair.

In therapy, Jenna learned to recognize that she was speaking to herself in a harsh and critical manner. While it was difficult to admit, she confessed that her negative thoughts were adding to her depression. I spoke to her about research showing that positive thoughts can reduce depression. Reluctantly, she agreed to try to speak to herself in a nicer way, even though she didn't believe the nicer thoughts were true. But in time, she saw that the new, kinder thoughts were helping her feel better and less hopeless. So, she continued with those thoughts. Eventually, Jenna was able to recognize that the voice of her harsh inner critic was actually a message she had received as a young girl from her mother, who had been highly critical and intolerant of her mistakes. Now, Jenna is able to talk back to the critic, let go of the burden of her mother's cruelty, and treat herself with greater self-respect.

Healing Strategy:
Cultivate Helpful Thoughts

This mindfulness practice invites you to become the compassionate witness of your thoughts, through which you build your capacity to nonjudgmentally and lovingly accept yourself.

You can do so using the structure of a meditation practice. Since a meditation practice can sometimes feel intimidating, you might choose to start slowly with, say, five minutes of practice a day. Set a timer so you do not need to look at the clock. Now, find a comfortable seated position. You can sit in a chair or a cushion on the floor—whatever allows you to sit comfortably for the next several minutes.

Now, begin to observe your thoughts with the intention of noticing whether each thought feels helpful or unhelpful. It is important here to note that we are not judging your thoughts as "good" or "bad." Rather, the invitation is simply to recognize the difference between thoughts that create greater ease and those that create distress.

The goal of this practice is to create clarity of mind. Give yourself permission to let go of any thoughts that create cloudiness or confusion. Unhelpful thoughts are unkind, unrealistic, over-generalized, self-diminishing, shaming, and filled with self-hate. They are often fueled by the inner critic. Other signs of unhelpful thoughts include harsh judgments of yourself or others and looping ruminations that fuel a feeling of hopelessness. Some examples of unhelpful thoughts might include:

- I am worthless.
- I am a failure.
- I'm a loser.
- I'll never get anything right.
- I will never get better.
- No one will ever love me.
- I cannot trust anyone.
- Nobody can live up to my standards.

As you explore the kinds of unhelpful thoughts that arise for you, notice if there are particular thoughts that keep coming back. Are they familiar? Perhaps ask yourself where and from whom you learned these negative messages about yourself or the world.

The next stage of this practice is to release those unhelpful thoughts and replace them with helpful and more accurate thoughts. Imagine that you are sitting on the bank alongside a river, sending forth unhelpful thoughts to continue downstream. Now, what new and helpful thoughts would you like to say to yourself instead? Here are some compassionate statements that you might try saying to yourself:

- I accept myself just as I am.
- I do not need to be perfect in order to be loved.
- I am enough just as I am.
- I deserve to be treated with kindness and respect.
- While I cannot trust everyone, I can find some people who are trustworthy.
- I am only human; I will be accepting of my mistakes.
- Other people are human; therefore, I will be accepting of their mistakes.

As you complete this practice, take a few moments to notice how you feel when you speak to yourself with kindness and accuracy. Do you notice any changes in how you feel emotionally? How do you feel in your body? Can you imagine how your behaviors might change as a result of this practice? Remember, repeated practice will help you create lasting change. Notice what happens when you experiment with the cultivation of helpful thoughts as a daily routine.

LEO

"I stopped having needs"

"My wife gets frustrated with me because I don't talk to her about my feelings. My problem is that most of the time, I don't know what I am feeling or what I want. When I was growing up, I wasn't able to talk to anyone and I certainly couldn't ask for anything. Either they ignored me or I was sent to my room. I guess I stopped having needs. She asked me to go to therapy because she feels I'm too distant; she thinks I'm depressed. I think that this is just who I am."

Ideally, caring parents help their children know that it is okay to have feelings by lovingly supporting them during moments of sadness, hurt, or anger. These types of interactions communicate to a child that it is okay to be vulnerable and that it is normal to have needs. In contrast, Leo's story is a powerful reminder of the painful consequences of childhood emotional neglect. His lack of parental support resulted in a void of inner awareness, an inability to recognize or articulate his feelings or needs.

In therapy, Leo spoke in a matter-of-fact tone, without any emotional expression on his face. Slowly, we began to turn toward the grief and loss of the young boy who had given up hope that anyone would ever really understand him or meet his needs for connection. Initially, this involved helping Leo identify when he was having feelings. We made space for the painful emotions of anger and sadness he felt toward his parents. He had spent many years in denial of his needs; however, we discovered that beneath his self-reliant disguise, Leo still had genuine needs for connection and love. He discovered that it was not too late; he could learn to feel his emotions.

Healing Strategy:
Embrace Your Emotions

Often, depressive symptoms arise because we have suppressed difficult emotions. This healing strategy, which is divided into two parts, focuses on helping you recognize and express your emotions. The first part involves recognizing feelings when they arise. This is especially important if your emotions were dismissed or disregarded in your childhood and if, as a result, you feel numb or cut off from your emotions. Somatic psychology teaches that you can learn to recognize emotions by focusing on bodily sensations. For example, you might notice that you feel tightness in your chest when angry, a lump in your throat when sad, or a feeling of contracting inward during times of shame. It may require a regular practice of checking in with your body before you start to make connections between your sensations and your emotions. In addition to building your own somatic awareness, it is valuable to have another person, such as a trained therapist, participate in this step. That other person can help you recognize the subtle shifts in your facial expressions or body language that can help you tune into your feelings.

You can explore your emotional self-awareness by bringing to mind a memory of a difficult event. Notice any changes in your bodily sensations. What do you imagine you were feeling during that difficult event? See if you can draw a connection between areas of tension in your body regarding an event and your emotions about that event.

Suppressing your emotions can worsen depressive symptoms. The next part of this healing strategy involves giving space to listen to, honor, and express your feelings. Let's take a closer look at how this might show up with some common emotions:

Anger: As discussed, depression is often anger turned inward. The benefit of feeling and expressing anger is that this emotion can give you the energy you need to free yourself from depressive symptoms. When sensing anger, you might notice a feeling of tightness in your chest and arms or a surge of energy in your belly or legs. Embracing anger in a healthy way might look like giving voice to the previously unexpressed feelings of betrayal, hurt, or rage that you have never expressed to an abuser. Suddenly you might have the energy to start exercising, which further boosts your mood. Or you can direct your anger into the completion of a project, which in turn increases your self-esteem. Anger is also an emotion that redirects your energy toward self-protection, which can help you define your boundaries or communicate your needs assertively.

Fear: Feelings of fear often involve trembling, shakiness, or a sense of being frozen. Often, we think that fear will go away if we just ignore it. However, suppressing fear tends to reduce access to your vitality, which can exacerbate depressive symptoms. Fear, like all emotions, needs to be felt so that you can access your courage. Sometimes you may feel fearful when remembering a frightening time from the past. Other times, you may be reacting to a threat in your current environment. If the fear is from your past, use your breath to find your courage: Feel your body, knowing that you can choose to come in and out of contact with the emotion. Remind yourself that you are safe now. If the feeling of fear is connected to your present circumstances, the emotion can help you courageously recognize the danger that surrounds you and make changes in your life to leave it.

Shame: Shame is a wound of not belonging. This emotion carries the burdens of rejection, humiliation, and betrayal. Moreover, shame often leads you to misbelieve that you were at fault. Shame often fuels depressive symptoms. You might feel an urge to isolate yourself and hide from the world. As intolerable as shame might feel, this emotion is directly connected to the underlying needs to be understood, cared for, unconditionally accepted, and loved. To embrace the emotion of shame, see if you can turn toward yourself in a kind, loving manner. Explore speaking to yourself the way you would reassure a young child, and allow the most vulnerable part of yourself to feel deeply cared for.

Sadness: Unexpressed feelings of hurt and sadness often underlie depressive symptoms. Sadness can be thought of as sacred access to your grief. See if you can look at your sadness with loving kindness. There is a difference between dwelling in sadness, which can turn into self-pity, and allowing your sadness to move through you. Every emotion is meant to be felt and to subside. Notice if you have a difficult time feeling your sadness or letting it go. Ultimately, a healthy expression of sadness involves allowing yourself to mourn for your losses and experiencing the healing power of your tears.

How Am I Doing?

Take a moment to review your experience of this chapter. Notice whether any of it has left you feeling unsettled or upset. If you need to, you can take breaks from this book. If you continue to have difficulty, remember that healing from C-PTSD is best supported through the compassionate care of a therapist. Depressive symptoms often are the result of accumulated experiences of powerlessness, hopelessness, and helplessness. It often takes time to feel relief from this accumulated pain. I recommend that you continue to replace judgmental or critical thoughts with compassionate self-talk. Likewise, I encourage you to embrace your emotions as a lifelong practice—one that not only unpacks emotional burdens from your past but also helps you to befriend difficult feelings on a regular basis. We will close this chapter with one final strategy focused on the healing power of movement.

Healing Strategy:
Stretch, Unwind, and Uplift

This final practice invites you to explore the movement of your body with gentle stretches and motions to release the physical heaviness and tension that often accompany depressive symptoms. If you have been inactive for quite a while, you might begin with gentle stretches. You might put on a favorite piece of music and stretch in your living room, or you might choose to go for a gentle walk outside. Or you may attend a yoga, tai chi, or Feldenkrais class in your community, which guides you through slow, mindful movement. If you would like, you can also explore vigorous movements. For example, you might walk at a faster pace, go for a run, or ride a bike. You might choose to attend a fitness class or go to the gym and lift weights. Notice how you feel as you increase your heart rate. Exercise provides you with a natural boost by increasing endorphins, our natural feel-good chemicals.

Remember to move at a pace that is right for you, and explore moving your body in ways that bring you joy. At the end of any movement practice, take a moment to appreciate yourself for enhancing your physical resilience. As with all the healing strategies in this book, I encourage you to return to this practice as part of your ongoing self-care routine.

5

Managing Emotional Dysregulation

"I Am Learning to Find Balance"

Many individuals who grew up in abusive or neglectful households have difficulty expressing emotions in a healthy way. Either they find themselves losing their temper, crying uncontrollably, and feeling out of control, or they shut down and feel cut off from their feelings. Both patterns are examples of emotional dysregulation that tend to disrupt the lives of individuals with C-PTSD. Within this chapter, we will discuss the origins of these types of symptoms. You will learn skills to help you develop a healthy and balanced relationship to difficult emotions. Moreover, these tools will allow you to enrich your inner life and enhance your capacity for joy.

CHRISTINE

"I get angry and can't stop myself from yelling"

"It all started because my husband told me that he has to go away for a business trip. Logically, I know that he loves me and that it's only a short trip. But I got this horrible feeling that he's going to leave me. I felt so out of control. Then, I got angry and couldn't stop myself from yelling. Afterwards, I felt so bad about myself. Now, I can't stop crying and I don't know what to do."

Christine walked into the office with tears rolling down her cheeks. She was caught in a web of emotional overwhelm and shame. We started our session by identifying the triggering event, which was learning that her husband was going away on a business trip. We explored the root of her fear of being left. As is often the case, we needed to look at the patterns of relationships in her childhood home.

Christine remembered how her mother would give her pretty dresses and dolls, although she didn't want or like those things. She just wanted her mother's love. When Christine refused to wear the dresses, her mother would scream at her and cry out, "Why don't you love me!" Afterwards, her mother would stop speaking to her, sometimes for days at a time.

As part of her healing, Christine practiced connecting to her "wise mind," a dialectical behavior therapy (DBT) concept that represents an integration of thinking and feeling. Intellectually, she recognized that her husband had no intention of leaving her. Emotionally, she felt unhinged. Through her wise mind, she was able to realize that her feelings were not about her husband—they were about her childhood. Christine was able to say, "I am learning to find balance with my strong emotions," as she felt more accepting of his need to go away for work. Now that she felt grounded, she was able to turn her attention to the pain of her childhood wounds.

Understanding Emotional Dysregulation

When you are emotionally regulated, you feel grounded and calm. You are able to compassionately accept that difficult feelings are an inevitable part of life. This allows you to express a range of emotions without feeling overwhelmed, numb, or reliant upon harmful behaviors. *Emotional regulation* permits you to make healthy decisions, advocate for your needs, and skillfully communicate with others. In contrast, *emotional dysregulation* refers to having strong reactions, such as uncontrollable sadness, rage, or fear, that disrupt your ability to focus at work, to parent your children, or to maintain loving relationships. Like Christine, you might have a fear of abandonment. Alternatively, you might feel triggered by someone else's behavior or feel distressed when someone you care about is disappointed with you. Emotional dysregulation often leads to behaviors you later regret. For example, you might take out your anger on another person or you might feel the urge to hurt yourself. These behaviors tend to increase to a downward spiral in which you feel consumed by self-hatred or start to think about suicide as the only way out of your pain.

Emotional dysregulation is common among survivors of childhood trauma. In part, this is because we learn how to regulate our emotions during childhood. Children require healthy, caring, and attentive adults to help them develop their social and emotional intelligence. It is the job of a parent to help children feel safe enough to express uncomfortable feelings. When children feel supported, they learn that stressful moments are only temporary and that they can resolve into positive experiences of empowerment or deepened connections in relationships. However, when parents are emotionally overwhelmed, they fail to help their children develop a healthy emotional landscape. Within this unsafe territory, children become explosive or cut off from their feelings. In some cases, children become hyper-aware of their parents' distress or are compelled to take care of their parents' emotional needs.

The Window of Tolerance

The patterns learned in childhood can come out in adulthood as a tendency to cry uncontrollably, get angry easily, feel lethargic and dull, or be overly attuned to the feelings of others. These patterns of emotional dysregulation indicate that you are outside your "window of tolerance," a term created by Dr. Dan Siegel to describe the range of stress that a person can manage without becoming overwhelmed. When you are inside this optimal zone, you are able to skillfully attend to upsetting emotions and distressing physical sensations. Inside your window of tolerance, you are able to handle a certain amount of stress and return to a sense of safety. However, when you are outside your window of tolerance, you might feel high-arousal emotions, such as fear, irritability, restlessness, anger, or excessive crying. These feelings mean that your sympathetic nervous system has kicked in. In contrast, low-arousal emotions mean that you are feeling a parasympathetic system response. You might feel fatigued, lethargic, helpless, emotionally dull, numb, or depressed. Often, those with C-PTSD alternate between these highs and lows.

Patterns of dysregulation learned in childhood often continue into adulthood. You might notice a tendency toward fight, flight, fawn, freeze, and faint responses. Let's take a closer look:

Fight: If you are prone to a fight response, you might feel critical of yourself and others or be angry or full of rage. You might have a strong need to feel in control. If you relate to this pattern, you may need to work with your anger in therapy, which can provide a healthy outlet for this emotion. Rather than taking this feeling out on yourself or others, you can use the energy of anger to set boundaries, feel empowered, or protect others who are being mistreated.

Flight: If you tend toward the flight response, you might notice a tendency to startle easily, feel hypervigilant to your surroundings, and be on guard. You might feel flighty, "caught in your head," have racing thoughts, or feel disconnected from your body. You may be fleeing from the reminders of the trauma. In this case, you may need to focus on slowing down, connecting to your body, and cultivating mindfulness of the here and now.

Fawn: When a child learns to cope by taking care of the parent's emotional needs, that child is relying on another defense structure, termed the "fawn" response by Pete Walker. The fawn response involves trying to appease or please a person who is a source of threat. The goal is to prevent an attack by caring for the emotional or physical needs of the abuser. This submissive response often results in a pathological attachment to the abuser (we discuss this topic in greater depth in chapter 9). In adulthood, an unresolved fawn response might lead to patterns of codependence, in which you sacrifice your own needs for the sake of maintaining relationships. If you struggle with the fawn response, it will be important to focus on developing your boundaries and improving your sense of self-worth.

Freeze: A freeze response happens when you become absolutely still in anticipation of your life being threatened. Think of a deer in a car's headlights. Often, there is a tendency to hold your breath, and you might feel frozen, like you cannot move your body. Just as an animal releases stress by shaking, moving, or breathing deeply, it often helps to explore healing movements to release from a freeze response.

Faint: The faint response happens when our bodies decide we are under threat and that we need to conserve energy in order to survive. With this response, you might feel disconnected, dissociative, numb, or have the urge to withdraw from others. Or you might experience nausea, dizziness, or difficulty with your vision. These symptoms indicate that you are relying upon a primitive defense system that kicks in when it senses that death may be unavoidable. To heal from a faint response, it is wise to slowly re-orient your attention toward your senses. For example, you can take a moment to look around your space and pay attention to any cues that help you feel relaxed and calm. Or, you might explore how it feels to connect with another person with whom you feel safe (we will discuss how to heal dissociative symptoms in greater depth in chapter 6).

Widening Your Window

Initially, trauma recovery focuses on building your capacity to feel resourceful and regulated. In other words, you learn how to stay within your window of tolerance. Once you feel better regulated, trauma recovery will help you expand your capacity to handle a wider range of emotional distress. This will assist you in widening your window of tolerance. In DBT, this process is called "increasing your distress tolerance." You can increase your window of tolerance by compassionately paying attention to uncomfortable emotions and bodily sensations while also recognizing that these feelings do not require knee-jerk reactivity. For example, you might notice a sense of irritability, a change in how you are breathing, a loss of focus, or that you suddenly become tired. Instead of pushing these feelings away, you can become curious. You might discover that these feelings are connected to the past. Maybe your body is letting you know that you need to make a change in your current circumstances. Now, instead of reacting impulsively, you can use positive coping strategies and choose wiser behaviors, such as setting a boundary, advocating for yourself, or mindfully ending an unhealthy relationship.

The imbalances of your autonomic nervous system have repercussions on your physical health. When you have been outside your window of tolerance for extended periods of time, you are more likely to have problems with digestion, sleep, your immune system, and your cardiovascular health. But you can also access the wisdom of your body to help you to heal. For example, if you were not able to protect yourself in a dangerous situation as a child, you can slowly and mindfully reclaim your ability to release your pent-up energy. In this way, you can support your health by connecting to movements that help you resolve traumatic situations that may have been stuck in your body for many years.

Start Healing Yourself

Take a moment to look over the earlier descriptions of the fight, flight, fawn, freeze, and faint responses. Do you see anything that seems similar to your own patterns of emotional response? Such self-awareness will be valuable as you work with the healing strategies provided in this section of the book. Here, we will explore some of the common experiences of symptoms of emotional dysregulation as described by Bonnie and Carl. The first healing strategy will help you build distress tolerance. The second healing strategy comes from somatic psychology and will help you access the healing power of your body. Remember that healing requires patience; I encourage you to reconnect to your emotions and sensations gently and do that at a pace that isn't overwhelming for you. You can broaden your capacity to be with discomfort, but it doesn't stop there. Your increased tolerance for distress and your use of embodiment—getting in touch with your physical sensations—can become the foundation for many positive changes, such as increased self-compassion and improvements in your relationships with others.

BONNIE

"I have to hold it all together or I'll fall apart"

"I started drinking and using drugs to cope when I was 12 years old. My parents were never around, so I found a way to deal with the pain. I felt so utterly alone. I had no friends at school; even my sisters left me out and barely talked to me. I got sober in my thirties, but I still struggle with the pain from my past. There are so many emotions held back behind a wall. I feel like I have to hold it all together or I'll fall apart."

Bonnie was afraid that if she felt her emotions, she would simply fall apart. Even though she had embraced sobriety, she was still struggling with her emotional pain. Now, she runs her own business and spends most of her time planning and organizing new projects. She pushes away her vulnerable feelings of shame and sadness by staying busy. Even though she is successful, she can spend hours worrying about her future.

In therapy, Bonnie described how she was either cut off from her feelings or consumed by emotional and physical pain. This "all or nothing" pattern was backfiring, though. She was ready to learn a new way of relating to her past. She learned to practice the DBT skill of building distress tolerance. Since, she had a pattern of disconnecting from her feelings, Bonnie needed to practice attending to her emotions and bodily sensations slowly and mindfully. Eventually, this helped her to recognize that she was strong enough to work through the pain of her childhood.

Healing Strategy:
Increase Your Distress Tolerance

An important goal of therapy is to learn how to handle painful emotions skillfully. It is important to learn how to be with difficult feelings, because no matter how hard we try, we can't avoid the challenges that come with being human. Often, when we feel uncomfortable sensations or emotions, they come with habitual thoughts, such as *Make it go away!* or *I can't handle this*. These thoughts can lead to self-harming behaviors, explosive emotional outbursts, or the urge to use substances.

Distress tolerance is a mindfulness practice. Once again, you can use the structure of a seated meditation. Set a timer for five minutes so that you do not need to look at the clock. Now, find a comfortable seated position in a chair or on a cushion on the floor. Begin to observe your sensations and emotions. If you notice an uncomfortable feeling, see if you can stay curious about your experience rather than acting on any urge to push the sensation or emotion away. It may help to remind yourself that all emotions are temporary.

Instead of judging your experience, try describing your sensory experience to yourself. Notice your temperature, areas of tension in your body, the feeling of this book in your hands, or the sensation of your breath. Observe what happens if you stay with your emotions just a little longer. Notice if there are any subtle changes that occur as you continue to breathe and observe your experience. Perhaps you find that the distress begins to subside as a natural consequence of your mindful, reflective awareness. Or you might see that you are able to turn toward the underlying emotions in a more conscious manner, one that allows for an experience of resolution.

CARL
"I feel so out of control"

"I am having a hard time with my three-year-old son. I know he's just being a kid and his behavior is normal. But I can't stand it when he refuses to do what I want him to do. Like, when we need to leave the house and he will not get in the car, or when it's time to go to bed and he won't go to sleep. When he cries, I feel so out of control. My body starts to shake and I just want to scream."

Carl was struggling with emotional dysregulation that was getting triggered when his son wouldn't do what he needed him to do. Thankfully, he was aware of this pattern and sought help before his emotional dysregulation became a problem for his son. Carl and I explored his feeling of being "out of control." As he grew curious about his emotional reaction, he recalled memories of being upset as a child. He described how his mother would become angry instead of providing a soothing or caring response. As a result, he internalized that his emotions were too much for anyone to handle.

The shaking and urge to scream that Carl described are symptoms of being in high arousal and outside his window of tolerance. These physical experiences were a direct connection to his own childhood emotions and attachment wound. More importantly, these same feelings helped Carl find resolution and heal from his past. By paying attention to his body, Carl was able to recognize that his urge to scream had more to do with his unexpressed anger toward his mother than to the immediate situation. Carl then noticed that his urge to scream at his son was subsiding. Now, he was able to engage his body to help him feel empowered so that he could be a loving parent for his son. He discovered that he could remain regulated and present during difficult moments with his son by taking deep breaths and focusing on his feet and legs in the midst of intense emotions.

Healing Strategy:
Engage and Empower

Somatic psychology invites awareness of how your body responds to triggering events. Rather than feeling stuck in high-arousal fight-or-flight responses, you can explore movements that allow you to release unnecessary tension so that you can feel present and empowered. In contrast, if you feel frozen or collapsed in freeze or faint responses, you can focus on engaging your senses and reconnecting to your breath, so as to help you feel an embodied experience of relaxed alertness. The following list provides ways that you can explore engaging your body when you feel emotionally overwhelmed or shut down. Practice each of these empowering movements mindfully and slowly. Repeat each movement two or three times, and then pause to notice any subtle changes in how you feel in your body and mind.

- Stand next to a wall and push your arms firmly into the wall. Press and release several times. Imagine that you are setting a boundary and pushing away anything that you do not want or that was a source of danger.

- While seated or standing, press your feet into the ground and engage the large muscles of your legs, and then relax. Firmly stand your ground, knowing that nobody can push you over.
- Stand up and walk slowly and mindfully in place. Imagine that you are leaving any situation that is not healthy for you.
- Stretch your arms out in front of you as if you are reaching out for something that is important to you. Notice how it feels to reach for what you want.
- Imagine grasping what you want in your hands and pull your arms back toward your chest. Explore how it feels to receive.
- When you experience any emotions, notice the accompanying sensations in your body. See how it feels to place your hands over these sensations, apply some light pressure, and take a deep breath.
- While sitting down, allow yourself to rest into your connection with your chair or couch. Notice if you feel an urge to collapse. If so, see if you can find enough muscular engagement to help you feel relaxed and awake.

How Am I Doing?

This chapter focused on emotional dysregulation. Now, I invite you take a moment to pause and reflect. Notice if anything in this chapter has you feeling activating or triggered. If so, try to remember that all the healing strategies in this book will become more accessible through repeated practice. If you continue to feel overwhelmed or shut down, remember that no book can replace a well-trained, trauma-informed therapist.

Your symptoms may be a sign for you to reach out for more support. In closing, this next healing strategy can help you reach a calm, connected, and centered part of yourself as you continue on your journey to trauma recovery.

Healing Strategy:
Access Your Inner Wisdom

Can you recall a time when you relied too heavily on your emotions when you had to make a decision? You might have felt moody, impulsive, or chaotic. In contrast, can you remember a time when you relied too much on thinking to reach a decision? In this case, you might later have second-guessed yourself or even talked yourself out of your true feelings. Perhaps, you can also think of a time when you felt both clear-headed and connected to your intuition. Accessing your inner wisdom is like walking a middle path—a balanced approach that takes into account your feelings and your logical reflections.

The psychotherapy model called Internal Family Systems refers to that inner wisdom as the "self"—the calm, confident, and compassionate core of who you are. Dialectical behavior therapy (DBT) refers to this as your "wise mind"—the quiet voice in you that simply knows what is right or true. Both these traditions use the tools of mindfulness to help you connect to your inner wisdom.

Accessing your inner wisdom also involves connecting with your embodied knowing. Even as you read these words, pause and notice the ways that your intuition communicates through your senses. Take a moment to reflect upon a current challenge that you are facing in your life. As you do so, listen for and sense the subtle changes in your belly, chest, or throat. Do you notice small changes in how you are breathing? Rather than overriding these signals, ask yourself, *What does my body want me to know?* Continue to experiment with this practice. Over time, see if you can discover how your body, mind, and emotions work together to help you access your inner wisdom.

6

Healing from Dissociative Symptoms

"I Am No Longer Afraid of My Past"

Dissociative symptoms can leave you feeling disoriented or disconnected from yourself and others. Dissociation is a learned behavior that helped you to survive and cope with the stress of ongoing trauma. You might continue to rely on dissociative symptoms to push away your pain. However, when left unresolved, these symptoms can become debilitating and can interfere with your ability to live a fulfilling, purposeful life. This chapter will help you increase your sense of safety now, so that you can turn your attention toward the pain of your past in order to heal it. In time, you will discover that you no longer need to deny or push away the reality of traumatic life events.

LENA

"If I didn't talk about it, I could pretend that it never happened"

∨

"I was 12 years old when my uncle molested me for the first time. I remember looking out the window. I felt so bad afterwards, like it was all my fault. I didn't tell my parents. The abuse continued for the next few years. It was so confusing. I liked my uncle, but I knew that what he was doing was wrong. I decided that if I didn't talk about it, I could pretend that it never happened. Now that I am in my fifties, I realize that not talking about it has been hurting me all these years. I am ready to heal."

Lena had been reading stories in the news of women and men coming forward and speaking about earlier sexual abuse. This helped her find the courage to come into therapy and share her story for the first time. While part of her was ready to heal, there was part of her that still wanted to deny the reality of what she had faced as a young girl.

In therapy, Lena learned to recognize how dissociation showed up in her life. She disconnected from her feelings and her body. Sometimes she would find herself staring blankly into space, only to find that 10 or 15 minutes had passed without her being aware of it. Lena began to use mindfulness to bring her awareness to her body. Initially, this process was painful. Some days, she felt that it was still easier not to feel anything. But over time, she increased her capacity to stay with the discomfort. She also discovered that there were benefits to staying connected to herself. She felt more empowered and connected to her intuition.

Now, Lena felt better prepared to talk about her past. When we looked more deeply at her history, I learned that her parents were rarely home—they were often out drinking. Lena coped the best way she could, and dissociation helped her push away feelings of confusion, fear, anger, shame, and disgust. In therapy, she began to work through the feelings connected to the abuse and eventually these events felt less disturbing. She declared, "I am no longer afraid of my past," and she described a feeling of empowerment. After completing therapy, Lena went on to work for an organization as an advocate for others who had experienced childhood sexual abuse.

Understanding Dissociative Symptoms

Many people incorrectly believe that dissociation is rare and only occurs if someone has suffered extremely serious traumatic events. When you read the word "dissociation," you might think that this refers to having multiple personalities, having lapses in memory, or experiencing "lost time." However, what most people do not realize is that dissociation exists on a continuum and that many of its symptoms are relatively common.

For example, dissociation can cause you to feel tired, foggy, forgetful, or distracted. Or, like Lena, you might feel disconnected from your body and "stuck in your head." Sometimes dissociation can lead you to feel like you are a child again, in which case you might feel young, lost, or little. You might feel as though your thoughts or actions are not your own. Or, depending on the severity of your symptoms, you might feel like your world is surreal, or you might arrive at places with no memory of how you got there. Most importantly, know that all dissociative symptoms once helped you survive ongoing stress and unresolvable threats.

Understanding the origins of your dissociative symptoms can strengthen your self-compassion and reduce any feelings of shame. From a physiological perspective, dissociation is linked to the faint response that we discussed in chapter 5. This happens when the parasympathetic nervous system is triggered. When you feel that there is no way to escape a threatening experience, it is common to feel immobilized, helpless, and despairing.

The faint response can also lead you to feel spacey, sluggish, and sleepy, owing to the body's release of naturally occurring opioids that have a numbing effect. People who are dissociated can also experience nausea, dizziness, a drop in blood pressure, a loss in the ability to speak clearly, or difficulty with vision. Heart rate and blood pressure can drop, sometimes rapidly, which can lead to actual fainting or psychogenic (non-epileptic) seizures, called vasovagal syncope. In addition to these physical conditions, those with C-PTSD can be prone to a wide variety of chronic-pain conditions and illnesses, owing to the dissociation from traumatic memories.

Dissociation and Memory

Dissociation can impair your ability to remember traumatic experiences accurately. This is because your brain goes into survival mode in situations where there is a high level of threat, such as during physical or sexual abuse. Memories of long-term facts and the sequential timing of events are created by the prefrontal cortex and hippocampus. In contrast, the amygdala is the area of the brain that maintains sensory and emotional details of memories. During traumatic events, bursts of adrenaline increase the blood flow to the amygdala, leading someone to form very strong memories of sensory fragments, such as smells, sounds, or bodily sensations. Simultaneously, the blood flow is reduced to those areas of the brain that are responsible for language, speech, learning, and long-term memory for facts. This is why you might recall certain sensory details, such as how you felt during an experience, but not remember exactly what happened or the chronological order of events. Additionally, you might find it difficult to talk coherently about your experiences with others.

When we experience trauma at birth or in early childhood, these memories can become strongly imprinted in the body and on the nervous system. Experts refer to memories from the first three years of life as "preverbal" memories because they formed before a child has developed language and speech. These memories are typically stored as motor patterns and sensations. (Another name for them is "body memories.") Preverbal memories hold the felt experience of a child's attachment relationships—those with the mother, father, or other childhood caregivers. If you experienced early childhood trauma, you might have strong emotions, bodily sensations, or dissociative symptoms without understanding why.

Dissociation as Defense

The traumatic events of childhood may have ended many years ago; however, dissociative symptoms often persist into adulthood. Psychologically, dissociation is a defense that helps you disconnect from the trauma of your past. Dissociation often involves other avoidance defenses (as discussed in chapter 2), such as overworking, emotional eating, or using substances. You may experience dissociation as a divide between the part of you that is able to carry out the demands of your life and the part that carries the pain of the past. As a result, you might feel "fine" when you are at work, while you parent your children, or when going to the store to buy groceries. But when you get home and are all alone, you might feel like a younger part of yourself. In these moments, you might feel as though the traumatic event is still happening, even though it ended many years ago. In some cases, you might have more complex dissociative divisions between multiple parts or alternate identities, in which you have no memory of how you arrived at places or of what you did there.

Dissociative symptoms often arise because someone feels it is impossible to acknowledge or fully realize the extensive emotional impact of past traumatic events. As discussed in chapter 1, trauma experts recommend that healing from C-PTSD be approached in stages. The first of these stages establishes safety and stabilization. During this time, it is helpful to cultivate compassionate self-awareness of your dissociative symptoms. The second stage involves confronting and working through traumatic memories. However, if you have dissociative symptoms, you might not feel ready to move toward trauma resolution and integration. In this case, you can focus on safety and stabilization for as long as you need.

It is important to know that you can heal, even if you cannot recall the details of your traumatic past. Here, somatic psychology can help by inviting you to focus on sensations and emotions, rather than on the details of the experiences. In fact, the goal of this therapy is to recognize that the traumatic events of your past are over now, so you can focus on your goals and hopes for the future.

Start Healing Yourself

In many ways, all the healing strategies offered in this book will help you to heal from the dissociative symptoms of C-PTSD. For example, developing mindfulness of the here and now (chapter 2), developing a peaceful place (chapter 2), connecting to your breath (chapter 3), embracing your emotions (chapter 4), and increasing your distress tolerance (chapter 5) all emphasize the first stage of healing, which is to establish safety and stabilization. I recommend that you continue to practice those healing strategies as often as needed.

The next two healing strategies focus on the second stage of healing from trauma and dissociation. The first of these strategies helps you build greater self-awareness of your dissociative symptoms. The second helps you work through traumatic memories safely and at a pace that is right for you. Notice how you feel as you read about Matt and Julie later in this chapter and how their chosen strategies helped them to heal. Remember, a book cannot replace a well-trained, trauma-informed therapist who is skilled in compassionately understanding and working with dissociation. It is a sign of health to seek support when you need it.

MATT

"I ran out of the theater into the parking lot, but I have no memory of it"

"It was Friday night and I went with a group of my friends to the movies. I was looking forward to a fun evening, but I didn't realize that the movie was going to be disturbing. There was this one scene about a man who killed himself. I guess I ran out of the theater into the parking lot, but I have no memory of it. A few of my friends came out to look for me, and told me about what I did. I don't understand what happened."

Matt was in his early twenties and had never been to therapy before. His behavior at the theater frightened him, and after talking it over with his mother, she encouraged him to get some help. As we explored Matt's history, I learned that his father had been diagnosed with depression and had taken his own life when Matt was only three years old. He didn't have any memory of the event, but he had been in the house when his father died. Matt had not only lost his father to suicide but his mother was also overwhelmed for several years afterwards.

After getting to know Matt's childhood history, we both became curious about his reaction to the movie. I asked him to imagine how he might have felt as a young boy around the time of his father's death. At first, Matt said that he couldn't feel a thing, but as he became mindful of his body, he noticed that he was holding his breath. He was able to recognize that the numbness and holding of his breath were both ways to stop feeling. In the coming weeks, he began to realize other ways that he disconnected from his feelings. In time, he was able to imagine how afraid and lonely he might have felt as a young boy. Eventually, Matt was able to stay connected to his body and emotions while talking about his father's death. He had integrated an important part of himself.

Healing Strategy:
Self-Awareness of Dissociative Symptoms

When you are healing from trauma, it is valuable to develop self-awareness of your dissociative symptoms. Remember, dissociative symptoms exist on a continuum, ranging from relatively mild to highly distressing. Without making any judgments, look at the following list and consider if you relate to any of these behaviors. You might choose to write about your experience of these symptoms in a journal. Most importantly, having an increased awareness of the early signs of dissociation can allow you to take better care of yourself before your symptoms worsen. Such early recognition can also permit you to employ other strategies from this book that help you feel grounded and safe. If you are in therapy, I also encourage you to discuss these symptoms with your therapist, as this can help the two of you work as a team to reach your health-care goals.

- I find myself staring into space or daydreaming.
- I have difficulty paying attention.

- I suddenly feel tired for no reason.
- I act differently when I'm in different situations or when I'm with different people.
- Sometimes I am confused about who I really am.
- Sometimes I feel, act, or talk like a younger person.
- I have a hard time remembering my childhood, even after the age of five.
- I feel like I am looking at the world through a fog.
- I feel numb or disconnected from my body and emotions.
- I get waves of nausea or dizziness.
- Sometimes the world feels strange or surreal.
- Sometimes I feel like I'm paralyzed and have difficulty moving.
- I arrive at places and don't know how I got there.
- I find things that I have bought, but I don't remember buying them.
- I have seizures or pain with no known medical reason.

JULIE

"I suddenly feel tired and the room starts to spin"

"I don't know what is wrong with me. I have a good life. I like my work and enjoy coming home and spending time with my dog. I should be grateful for what I have. But there are times when I suddenly feel tired and the room starts to spin. My doctor told me that he cannot find any medical reason for my vertigo. He suggested that I go to therapy. None of this makes sense to me."

Julie's physical symptoms were concerning and confusing to her. At first, she wasn't convinced that therapy would make any difference. However, we began to explore her childhood history for clues about her mental and physical health. It didn't take long until she noticed an improvement in her health.

Julie described an ideal childhood. Her parents were well regarded in their community, and she was the oldest of four children. They were well dressed, attended church every Sunday, and were always well behaved. However, what Julie had never spoken about was the stress in her home behind closed doors. Her father was very strict and her mother was often overwhelmed with the challenge of maintaining an orderly household. As the oldest child, Julie was often responsible for her younger siblings. She grew up too quickly, without a chance to play, get messy, feel sad, or be angry. She felt weighed down by the need to be perfect.

When Julie would feel dizzy, foggy, or tired in our sessions, we paid close attention to these experiences. She began to notice that they were accompanied by feelings of sadness, hurt, and a deep longing for connection. As we reflected upon her childhood, she recalled moments that she had really wanted her mother's or father's attention as a little girl, but had to suppress her needs for connection. She didn't want to rock the boat. We realized that her emotional needs had been pushed down, held in her body for many years. Now, there was enough space for her to finally be herself.

Healing Strategy:
Develop Dual Awareness

Dual awareness strategies are used by both EMDR therapy and somatic psychology as a tool for safely working through traumatic memories. These strategies involve paying attention to cues that you are safe, while you are simultaneously reflecting upon a challenging memory. If you tend to have dissociative symptoms, dual awareness is an essential skill that can reduce any overwhelming feelings when you are thinking about traumatic memories.

To develop dual awareness, you will alternate your attention between your awareness of the present moment and your awareness of a difficult moment from the past. It is wise to find a supportive therapist before considering your most distressing childhood wounds. However, you can start to build the skill of dual awareness by beginning practice with relatively benign recent stressful events. Start slowly by committing to this practice for five minutes at a time. Set a timer so you do not need to look at the clock.

To begin this practice, find a place where you know that you are safe and feel at ease. Take a moment to look around your space and notice any cues that help you feel relaxed and calm. Now, think of a recent time that was stressful for you. Notice the sensations in your body and the emotions you feel. Pay attention to any differences in how you are breathing or any changes you make in your posture. After a few moments, put aside the stressful memory and bring your awareness back to your surroundings. Take a deep breath and let go of any lingering distress. Focus your attention on the here and now until you feel relaxed and calm. Now, mindfully alternate your attention between the stressful memory and the safety cues.

As you complete this practice, check in with your body. Are you noticing any shift in your ability to reflect upon a stressful moment, while also being able to return to a sense of ease and calm? This may not happen the first time you explore this strategy, but revisit the practice and increase the length of time you spend exploring the dual awareness. Over time, notice if it is easier to return to a sense of safety during stressful moments in your life.

Even small stressors can trigger dissociative symptoms or can lead to being flooded with emotions. If at any point you feel overwhelmed, it is wise to honor your symptoms, stop this practice, and return to the healing strategy "Reclaim Choice" from chapter 1 (see page 22).

How Am I Doing?

This chapter has focused on helping you understand the dissociative symptoms of C-PTSD. Take a moment to reflect now. Could you relate to the stories? Has anything in this chapter left you feeling distressed? If so, you can return to any of the other healing strategies in this book at any time. Or you might find it beneficial to seek support from a caring, trauma-informed therapist. Finally, the next healing strategy will help you work with your parasympathetic nervous system and vagus nerve to create a sense of balance and calm.

Healing Strategy:
Nourish Your Nervous System

You can access the healing power of your vagus nerve through your social nervous system, the most recently evolved circuit of the vagus nerve which helps us to feel safe and connected. This will help you to manage your parasympathetic nervous system so as to remain calm when you start to feel distressed. It is important that you do this practice at a time when and in a place where you feel safe. Take your time with each step and notice how you feel.

- Listen to a soothing piece of music and hum along to stimulate your vagus nerve.
- Bring one hand over your heart and one hand over your belly, and take several deep breaths.
- Bring your hands lovingly over your face and head. Gently touch your cheeks or move your hands over the top of your head. Imagine that you are touching the face of a dear friend or a child with loving care.
- Engage your sense of smell with an essential oil that brings a positive feeling.
- Reflect on a memory of a time when you felt connected and loved. Allow yourself to relax into the positive feelings of the memory.
- Snuggle with a pet, stuffed animal, or soft blanket.
- Call a caring friend and savor the experience of being connected.

7

Cultivating Healthy Interpersonal Relationships

"I Am Learning to Trust Myself and Others"

In this chapter, we will explore the interpersonal problems common among those with C-PTSD. Childhood trauma can lead to ineffective relationship patterns, such as blaming, criticizing, or unnecessarily withdrawing from loved ones. You might experience difficulty in feeling close to others. Or, in contrast, you might feel afraid of being alone. Experiences of childhood abuse or neglect can lead you to have difficulty asserting yourself or maintaining healthy boundaries. In this chapter, you will learn strategies that will help you turn toward feelings of hurt or rejection with greater self-compassion. You will also explore how to handle interpersonal conflicts more effectively. As a result, you can cultivate meaningful connections and satisfying relationships.

"I have a hard time making decisions. I get so focused on what other people want that I lose touch with myself. Even if I do know what I want, I am scared to tell my boyfriend. I just can't handle any more rejection. That's when I pull away from him, and I know he gets confused about why I stop responding to his calls."

When Jennifer came into therapy, she described feeling lost and dissatisfied in her relationship. Together, we began to explore how these feelings related to her childhood. She shared a memory about being a little girl and asking her mother for help. She recalled how her mother looked at her and laughed. This one memory represented the many times she felt shamed for having needs as a child. She became very observant of her mother's facial expressions and body language. Jennifer learned to be a "good" girl in order to avoid disappointing her mother.

As we worked together, therapy helped strengthen Jennifer's sense of herself as an adult, so she could feel more grounded and resourceful in her relationship. She began to feel a greater sense of compassion for the pain she experienced as a young girl. She gained a greater understanding as to why she would lose touch with herself and why it was difficult for her to express her needs to her boyfriend. Now, she was able to focus on asserting her needs, even if this meant risking feelings of rejection. Jennifer also recognized that she could advocate for herself by asking her boyfriend for moments of loving connection when she felt afraid. The feeling of safety began to extend into other relationships with friends and coworkers. With a feeling of satisfaction and a big smile on her face, she shared, "I am learning to trust myself and others."

Understanding Interpersonal Problems

It is often difficult for people with C-PTSD to develop healthy, lasting relationships. You may have little or no history of actually having safe and nurturing people in your life. It may also be harder to see people as safe and nurturing, even when they are. As is the case with Jennifer's story, growing up with childhood trauma and attachment wounds can impact your ability to form meaningful, satisfying connections with others.

Relationship problems can take many forms. For example, if you had an unpredictable or abusive parent, you might have coped by taking care of that parent's needs in order to avoid punishment, rejection, or abandonment. Or, you might have learned to withdraw from connection by becoming overly self-reliant. Either way, you might wrongly believe that you were at fault—that you were the cause of your abuse or neglect. This can develop into low self-worth and the belief that you are unlovable or a burden. Deep down, you might believe that you deserve to be treated poorly.

Having a history of childhood trauma can make you more prone to misperceiving the intentions and emotions of others. For example, you might think that your partner is angry with you when, in fact, the person is actually upset about an unrelated event, such as one that happened at work. Or, you might feel worried that your partner will be unfaithful, even though the individual has consistently been trustworthy and caring. Sometimes it can be difficult to separate current circumstances from the pain of your past. This can lead to defensive reactions that can be confusing to you and to your loved ones.

Intimate Relationships

Childhood trauma can lead to difficulties with emotional and sexual intimacy with partners. You might have issues receiving loving touch from a partner, or you might feel the urge to run away from a loved one who wants to be close to you because it brings up memories of being abused as a child. You might feel fearful of abandonment and irrationally jealous during times of normal, healthy separation. You might override your own boundaries physically or emotionally to avoid disappointing others or develop patterns of codependence, which can result in your sacrificing your own needs for the sake of the relationship. In some situations, you might notice damaging patterns in intimate relationships in which you lash out in hurtful ways toward others or you overlook "red flags" about partners who are abusive, dismissive, or rejecting.

Parenting

Interpersonal difficulties can also arise when parenting children. For example, if you did not feel loved or understood as a child, you might feel irrationally jealous of your child when he or she gets appropriate nurturance and care. Or you might feel resentful when your child says no, especially if you felt unable to assert yourself and your needs when you were a child. It is common to feel triggered by a child's dysregulated emotions, especially if the child is acting aggressively. However, if you notice that you are getting activated to the point of wanting to yell at or hit your child, it is important to walk away until you feel grounded and regulated. If these feelings arise frequently, it is wise to seek therapeutic support.

Friends and Colleagues

The childhood wounds of neglect and abuse can make it difficult to develop satisfying relationships with friends and coworkers. You might find it hard to set boundaries, or you might isolate yourself by declining social invitations. You might hesitate to assert yourself when speaking with a boss or become flooded with performance anxiety when you are asked to speak in public. Such social anxieties are often fueled by a severe sense of self-criticism that makes you believe others are judging you when they are not. You might be so convinced that other people will reject you that you inadvertently push them away. When they leave, then, you might use the evidence of abandonment to prove to yourself that you are unlovable.

When your trauma has been interpersonal in nature, connecting with another person can feel deeply threatening—so much so that you might not feel it possible to reclaim any faith in genuine human kindness. If you have been profoundly hurt by people in your past, it can take time to learn that there are some people who are trustworthy and kind. In truth, it is not easy to face painful memories of times when you were abandoned or times when you were violated by another person. It takes great courage to risk the pain of further rejection. However, it is a universal birthright to be loved, and should you desire it, it is possible to create healthy, loving relationships with partners, children, friends, and your community at large. You can learn to feel securely attached as an adult, even if you didn't have secure attachment as a child.

Start Healing Yourself

In this section, you will read about Patricia and John, and the way interpersonal problems impacted their lives. You will also learn healing strategies drawn from parts-work therapies that helped Patricia and John cultivate healthier patterns in their relationships. These practices will help you strengthen your connection to your adult self, so as to compassionately attend to the vulnerable feelings held by a younger part of yourself. Remember, it is wise to try these practices slowly or to explore these parts-work practices within a caring, therapeutic relationship. If at any point you find these practices to be distressing, you can always skip this section and find healing strategies in other areas of this book that help you to feel grounded.

PATRICIA

"The feeling reminds me of how I felt as a little girl"

"When I am home alone with my two young children, I start to feel panicky. I feel terrified that I will get trapped. The feeling reminds me of how I felt as a little girl, when my mother would lose her temper with me and my sister. She was so angry and I couldn't get away."

Patricia's story is a reminder of how common it is to have your own childhood trauma evoked while you are parenting your children. You might feel like a younger version of yourself. In these moments, you might feel insecure or have scary feelings connected to memories from your past. Using the next healing strategy, Patricia learned to strengthen her awareness of her adult self so that she could access her coping resources. As a result, Patricia was better able to feel grounded and was less triggered by the experience of being alone with her children.

Healing Strategy:
Anchor Your Adult Self

Unresolved traumatic events from childhood are often held in memory by a young part of the self. This is commonly referred to as your inner child. At times, you might feel identified with this young part of you that feels small or insecure. This healing strategy comes from parts-work therapy as a tool to connect to your adult self. As an adult, you have a range of choices that weren't available to you as a child. Being anchored in your adult self can help you recognize that those events of your past are over now. This healing strategy is particularly helpful when you are experiencing flashbacks. You do not need to approach these practices in a specific order; experiment and discover what works best for you.

- Look at your hands and notice that these are the hands of an adult.
- Stand up and feel how tall you are by reaching toward the top of a doorframe. Recognize that you are the height of an adult.

- Take a look at a clock and a calendar. Notice the current time and date as a way to orient yourself to the here and now.
- Think of two or three things that you are able to do in your life now that were not possible when you were a child (e.g., driving a car, going to work).
- Say to yourself, *I know that I am an adult now and that I am safe. I am in charge of my choices and behaviors.*

JOHN

"I have never felt confident in social settings"

"I see how easy it is for other people to get out there and make friends. But for me, I feel so different. I'm reminded of being in school as a kid and how I was bullied. I have never felt confident in social settings. At some point, I just stopped trying. I just know that there is something wrong with me."

John's story is a reminder that childhood trauma can take a toll on your capacity to maintain meaningful relationships in a variety of social settings. Not only was John bullied in school but also his parents never helped him work through the impact of those experiences. They weren't emotionally available to support him. His mother was often anxious and his father was disengaged at home because he worked much of the time. John coped by working hard at school, but he had a hard time making friends. Now that he is in college, John sees others making friends easily and he wishes he could feel more confident. Sadly, he has become increasingly isolated.

In therapy, John was able to build greater self-awareness about the impact of his childhood trauma and neglect. For the first time, he was able to feel his emotions of anger and hurt. We explored what it would have been like as a child to have had supportive, protective, and loving parents. We discussed how it might have felt to have a mother who didn't collapse into tears when John talked to her about his own difficulties. He imagined having a father who paid attention to him, believed in him, and helped him learn to stand up for himself against the bullies at school. As John imagined these healing experiences, he explored how his life might have been different. Over time, he felt increasingly empowered to initiate friendships and attend social events at school. He began to feel more comfortable beginning conversations with others, and he noticed that they responded positively and invited him to participate in other events. He was rebuilding his social identity.

Healing Strategy:
Imagine a Reparative Experience

In order to heal from C-PTSD, it is important to acknowledge the pain that you felt as a child. This next healing strategy allows you to imagine new healing or reparative experiences that can help you develop a nurturing relationship with your younger self. For example, if you felt alone or neglected as a child, you imagine a nurturing person who could have been there with that young part of you. If you felt afraid or threatened, then a reparative process might involve bringing in a new experience of protection. If you were being abused or violated, your reparative experience might involve leaving the dangerous environment or being rescued. Or, if you felt humiliated and ashamed, your reparative process could involve imagining an experience of being accepted. But if you are currently feeling triggered, start by strengthening your adult sense of self by using the previous healing strategy, "Anchor Your Adult Self" (see page 107).

Begin this practice by imagining a specific event from your childhood that continues to feel painful to you. Take some time to visualize this event, and imagine how you felt back then. If you were to look at a photograph of yourself from this time, what would you see in your face? What else might you notice? Now, take the time to reflect upon what was missing in the experience. What was it that you most needed then? What do you imagine your young self needed to hear? For example, did you need to be nurtured, protected, rescued, fully accepted, or something else?

Now, can you imagine meeting the needs of your young self? Perhaps you can imagine visiting your childself as the adult you are now, or imagine another person whom you would like to have had there with you. Take time to imagine giving healing words or actions to yourself as a child. What do you notice now? How do you feel emotionally and in your body?

Take about 10 minutes to explore this healing moment. Know that you can repeat this process as often as you want by returning to this memory, until your younger self feels soothed. If you notice that it is difficult to cultivate compassion or loving-kindness for the painful memories of your past, remember that it can be helpful, when healing childhood trauma, to work with a caring therapist. But if this strategy brought you relief, you can choose to repeat this process with other memories.

How Am I Doing?

This chapter focused on healing the interpersonal wounds of your past in order to help you develop healthy interpersonal relationships in the present. Remember, relationship problems are at the very center of C-PTSD and childhood trauma. It is important to be gentle with yourself, especially when you are in conflict with loved ones. Interpersonal challenges may continue to arise throughout your life. However, the impact of these difficult moments will be less intense as you practice speaking kindly and repairing the difficult moments as they arise. The final healing strategy of this chapter invites you to practice skills that foster healthy relationships in your life now.

Healing Strategy:
Practice Healthy Relationship Skills

When you feel triggered in relationships, it is common to feel the urge to lash out at a loved one or cut off that connection. These strategies do not help you to work through difficult moments, however. The following list offers some suggestions for navigating conflicts with friends, coworkers, and partners. You don't need to use these skills in a specific order. Experiment and discover what works best for you and your relationships.

- If you are feeling triggered, walk out of the room and count down from 10 to 0 to let go of an urge to yell, criticize, put down, or hit another person.

- Observe your experience and name your feelings out loud to the other person. For example, you might say, "Right now, I am feeling . . . [angry, sad, scared]." Notice how the experience changes when you acknowledge your emotions to others.
- Take the time to ask questions of others so as to communicate your interest in their thoughts, feelings, and needs.
- Express yourself with confidence by maintaining eye contact and fine-tuning your posture so that you keep your spine straight and heart open.
- Explore how it feels to communicate assertively about what you want or do not want in the relationship.
- Recognize that others may say no, and that is okay.
- Avoid making judgmental, accusatory, or critical comments about others.
- Explore assertively setting boundaries by saying no if someone asks something of you that doesn't feel right.
- You can always take breaks from difficult conversations, though it's a good idea to make an agreement to come back to the conversation when you feel calm.
- Take the initiative to repair a difficult moment with a loved one by acknowledging when you have spoken or behaved hurtfully.
- Tell yourself and others that it is okay to make mistakes. You do not have to be perfect, nor do others.

8

Healing Self-Perception Issues

"Now I Realize that It Was Never My Fault"

In this chapter, we discuss how C-PTSD can affect your self-perception and sense of self-worth. Experiences of abuse or neglect often lead to self-blame and feelings of shame, in which you believe that you are at fault, damaged, unworthy, or a failure. In order to heal, it is important to work with your self-perception issues—mentally, emotionally, and physically. With practice, you can reclaim a positive sense of your self-worth.

SEBASTIAN

"I deserved everything that happened to me"

"Sure, my dad hit me. But I was such a difficult kid. I deserved everything that happened to me!"

Sebastian worked hard in the construction business to support his family. He was a responsible husband and father. But when he would get triggered, he would attack himself verbally. These self-attacks were especially fierce if he felt he had made a mistake. Then he would say, "I'm such a loser! I can't get anything right! What is wrong with me?" Sometimes, he would turn these critical statements toward his wife and daughter, which made him just feel worse about himself. That is when he'd call himself a monster.

It was his wife who encouraged Sebastian to come to therapy. She knew that he hadn't had an easy childhood, and she felt sad to see him be so hard on himself. In therapy, we explored Sebastian's history. He described himself as a tough kid. He had a hard time in school and was never a good student. He spoke about how his father would smack him around when he misbehaved or got bad grades. This started happening when Sebastian was pretty young. By the time he was a teenager, he had gotten involved with the "wrong crowd" and started drinking and getting into fights.

At first, Sebastian was convinced that his father had done nothing wrong. He said that he deserved to be hit because he was a difficult kid. However, we began to explore this harsh inner critic and we discovered that he was actually carrying an immense amount of shame. Not only had his father treated him harshly but also his mother had never stepped in to protect him. As a result, he assumed he must have deserved it. Sebastian's self-critical thoughts were his way of turning the anger he felt toward his parents inward on himself.

Once he recognized this pattern, Sebastian was able to talk about his feelings. He recognized that he had defended himself against vulnerable emotions because it had not been safe to reveal that he had felt hurt when he was a child. Sebastian shared, "Now I realize that it was never my fault." In time, he became more self-accepting, tolerant of his mistakes, and emotionally available to his wife and daughter.

Understanding Self-Perception Issues

As we see in Sebastian's story, a history of childhood trauma can lead someone to struggle with self-perception, often developing a sense of self that is based on the inaccurate belief that the individual is damaged, inferior, worthless, or unlovable. These beliefs often come with feelings of shame and guilt. It is common to feel as though you do not belong or that you are very different from other people. Difficulties with self-perception can also lead you to mistakenly believe that other people are rejecting or criticizing you.

Challenges in self-perception are common in abusive households. Children may believe that the abuse or neglect is their fault, because it can be too frightening for them to face the fact that they have a threatening parent or caregiver. A child is completely dependent upon his or her caregivers. The child's very survival requires that he or she make a dangerous environment tolerable, even if just in fantasy. For instance, a child might create an idealized mommy or daddy to avoid facing the reality of abuse and may carry the burden of being the "bad" child in order to avoid the terrifying reality that there is a "bad" parent.

Feelings of shame or unworthiness can also arise as the result of an accumulation of small and subtle rejections that occur on a daily basis. For example, you might have felt rejected when you excitedly reached out for connection to a parent, who then responded with disinterest. Or, maybe you came home from school with a special piece of art made for mommy, but later you discovered your creation had been thrown in the trash. When our needs for connection are repeatedly denied, it is common to feel angry and sad. In a healthy relationship, these emotions are recognized and received as part of a repair process. However, as discussed in chapter 7, when there is childhood trauma, there is often no acknowledgment or repair of these painful moments of dis-connection. These unresolved experiences of betrayal tend to accumulate and influence your sense of self.

It can be difficult to tolerate the discomfort of shame, anger, and hurt that often accompanies childhood trauma. An adult survivor may struggle with perfectionism, unrelenting self-criticism, and addictions. For example, you might react angrily toward others or become hypercritical of yourself in order to avoid feeling sad. Ultimately, it is important to make space for your vulnerable feelings, either in therapy or by using the healing strategies offered in this book. In doing so, you can learn to be with your emotions without the need to run away, attack yourself, or attack others.

Self-perception issues also present in your body. For example, feelings of worthlessness can shape how you carry yourself through the world, affecting your posture, facial expressions, or readiness to make eye contact with others. Chronic pain and illness are also common for people with C-PTSD. You might feel as though your physical symptoms mean that you are damaged or broken.

Healing involves recognizing that your feelings of shame or unworthiness are directly connected to your undeniably legitimate human needs for connection. Furthermore, since shame is an interpersonal wound, healing often needs to occur within a relationship. Initially, this may happen in therapy, but eventually it is important to feel that you are being treated fairly and respectfully in your other relationships. You can learn that, even though you have been rejected by some people, you can still seek out others who can meet your needs for connection. You can find people who are capable of meeting you with enthusiasm, even if you weren't celebrated as a child.

Start Healing Yourself

In this section, you will discover healing strategies to work with self-perception issues mentally, emotionally, and physically. We will look more closely at shame and self-doubt through Rebecca's story and explore a DBT-based validation strategy. Mariah's story highlights the physiological impact of C-PTSD symptoms, and it reminds us that we can feel the emotion of shame as heaviness and physical discomfort in our entire body. Her story is followed by a healing strategy based in somatic psychology that focuses on using the tension in your body as an essential part of trauma recovery.

REBECCA

"I have such a hard time validating my own feelings"

"Every time I try to tell my girlfriend how I feel, she puts me down or makes me feel like I'm wrong. The problem is that I start believing her. It's like I keep waiting for someone else to affirm my experience. I have such a hard time validating my own feelings."

Rebecca came to therapy because she was having a hard time in her relationship. She felt insecure and was constantly questioning herself about what she was doing wrong. As we explored her experience, she shared that she often made plans with friends and then cancelled at the last minute. When she tried to speak to her girlfriend about her feelings, she would react defensively and turn the conversation around to blame Rebecca for any problems they were having.

We started to explore her childhood history, and I learned that she had grown up with a mother who was jealous and critical of her. Rebecca realized that her current relationship was similar to the experiences she had as a child. Therapy helped Rebecca imagine how it might feel for her experiences and emotions to be validated. She learned to validate her own emotions outside of therapy. As she felt stronger, she was no longer willing to tolerate how her girlfriend treated her. Initially, she set clear boundaries about how she wanted to be treated; however, she soon realized that her partner was not capable of meeting her needs, so she ended the relationship. She gained clarity of her own self-worth and she felt ready to find a partner who was capable of giving her the love she deserved.

Healing Strategy: Validating Emotions

We receive validation when someone listens to us without judgment. That person is offering unconditional acceptance, which allows us to acknowledge the importance of our thoughts and feelings. This DBT-inspired healing strategy focuses on helping you validate your own emotions by offering unconditional acceptance of your own experience. Explore the following suggestions during times of intense or distressing emotions and experiences. This practice can be especially helpful during times when you feel confused or unclear about your response to a person or situation. Remember, if you find self-validation challenging, it is okay to seek support from someone you trust.

- See if you can identify the difficult emotion that you are feeling. Is it sadness, anger, fear, disappointment, confusion, or shame?
- Notice any judgmental or invalidating thoughts you are having, such as *I'm being too sensitive, I should just get over it,* or *My feelings are stupid.*
- Make an agreement with yourself to suspend or stop any invalidating thoughts. Try saying to yourself the word *Stop* and then saying, *I deserve to treat myself with kindness and respect.*

- Try to find the source of the difficult emotion by asking yourself, *When did I first start feeling this way?* or *What circumstances contributed to my feelings?*
- Explore validating statements such as "My feeling makes sense because . . ." or "How I feel is important because . . ."
- If it is difficult to validate your experience, ask yourself, *How would someone else feel in my situation?* Explore how you would offer compassion to that person.
- Ask yourself, *What do I want?* and then tell yourself, *If it is important to me, then it is important.*
- Notice what happens as you acknowledge and accept your current experience and emotional response. How do you feel in your body now?

MARIAH

"I don't know if I can go on like this"

"I am in so much pain. There are days I am so tired that I can hardly get out of bed. I don't know if I can go on like this. Sometimes, I think that I should never have been born."

Mariah lived with physical health challenges and a pervasive feeling of hopelessness. She was under medical care for chronic fatigue; however, her doctors suggested that she also seek therapy to deal with the impact on her body of her childhood trauma. As we explored her history, I learned that she had been raised by a single mother who was profoundly rejecting of her. Her mother often told her that she never wanted children and that she regretted the day that Mariah was born. Now in her forties, Mariah felt the crushing weight of her unresolved pain.

Unresolved emotions related to trauma can get held in the body. Feelings of shame or unworthiness can show up as a caving in of your chest, a collapse in your posture, and a lowered head and gaze. Over time, this posture can further contribute to a diminished sense of yourself that reinforces self-perception problems. In therapy, Mariah was able to talk about her childhood; however, she felt disconnected from her body and still struggled with crippling exhaustion.

It was important to help her move beyond the words of her story and to access the ways in which the trauma was held in her body. Healing involved slowly and safely connecting to her body. Initially, attending to her body was a challenge. She felt as though her body had betrayed her. When she focused on her sensations, she would become flooded with feelings of shame and a belief that she was unlovable. With practice, though, Mariah discovered that when these painful feelings arose, she could place her hands over her heart and focus on an intention of loving herself. She felt a combination of grief and relief as she slowly opened to this new sense of self-compassion.

Mariah continued to explore her pain and fatigue symptoms as they arose. She learned to mindfully increase her awareness of her bodily sensations. This helped her move and breathe in a way that supported the tension in her lower back, shoulders, and neck. Each time she focused her attention on her body, she would have an emotional release that would lead to temporary relief from her physical symptoms. She began to feel hope for her future for the first time in her life.

Healing Strategy:
Somatic Release Practices

This healing strategy offers an opportunity to release physical tension by inviting you to focus your attention on the common places that trauma gets held in the body. As with all the healing strategies in this book, explore this practice mindfully and slowly. Remember that you can take a break or move to other healing strategies if you feel overwhelmed at any time. The following list does not need to be done in any specific order, nor are these the only areas of your body that might carry tension. I encourage you to explore one area of your body at a time, knowing that you can return to this practice as often as you need.

In this practice, you will bring your hands over an area of your body and focus your breath beneath your hands to enhance your awareness of sensations in that area. Start by focusing on each area of your body for one to two minutes. You can increase the time you spend on this healing strategy if you find it to be helpful. As much as possible, make room for your emotions as you breathe into your somatic awareness.

You might notice that your body shakes or trembles as you release emotional tension. If this happens, follow any movement impulses that help you release the tension. For example, you might shake out your arms and legs. In addition, the following prompts invite you to explore some common emotional themes related to each area of the body. You might relate to these themes; however, it is important that you pay attention to and honor your own experience.

Throat, neck, and jaw: Tension in the throat may be connected to times that you didn't speak your truth. Is there a sound that matches the feeling of tightness in your jaw? Perhaps you can explore how it feels to open and close your mouth or stick out your tongue. Can you give yourself permission to have your voice now?

Upper back and shoulders: Tension in your shoulders or upper back might be related to carrying emotional burdens or feeling like you need to hold the weight of the world. What might it feel like to let these burdens go? If you have been feeling stressed about your to-do list, can you acknowledge what you have accomplished and realize that it is "good enough"?

Chest, heart, and lungs: Tension in the chest, heart, and lungs can sometimes be connected to feelings of loss and grief. Do you have any losses or hurts that need your attention? Can you breathe in a way that moves emotional tension out of this area of your body?

Belly, stomach, and intestines: Tension in the belly, stomach, and intestines can correspond to events in your life that are difficult to emotionally or mentally digest. Feelings of nausea or disgust can be an indication that your boundaries were invaded. Notice how your body responds when you reflect upon experiences that were not safe or nurturing. Explore how your body feels when you recall times you felt cared for.

Lower back, hips, and pelvis: Holding tension in your lower back, hips, or pelvis might be connected to feelings of fear. Perhaps you feel as though you are in survival mode or are unsure about your right to exist. As you breathe into these areas of your body, focus on the cues that remind you that you are safe now.

How Am I Doing?

As we come to the end of this chapter, take some time to reflect on your self-perception. Did you relate to the stories? Has anything in this chapter left you feeling distressed? It is important to remember that feelings of shame and unworthiness are extremely common. These feelings can serve as a reminder to take a moment for self-care.

The final healing strategy focuses on paying attention to positive moments of feeling loved or nurtured, which can support you in healing from shame.

Healing Strategy:
Recall a Loving Moment

Begin this practice by placing one or both hands over your heart. Allow your breath to slow down as you take several deep belly breaths. Now, take some time to reflect upon a time in which you felt loved by someone—a time in which you felt safe in a relationship. Maybe, this was with a good friend, a teacher, a therapist, a family member, or even a pet. If you are able to recall such a time, take your time to enhance your memory of this positive and loving moment. Where were you when this positive event occurred? How old were you at the time? What do you recall seeing in the eyes of this person, or what did you hear in the person's voice? If it is a pet, can you recall the feeling of contact with their fur or the sensory experience of connection?

Now, what are you aware of in your body? Can you sense any warmth or a feeling of relaxation? What emotions are you feeling? Bring your attention back to the sensation of your hand over your heart. Continue to focus on any positive emotions of love and safety, and allow these feelings to grow. Linger here as long as you like.

Remember that when feelings of shame or unworthiness arise, you can return to this memory of a loving moment as often as needed. Each time you reorient your attention from difficult memories to positive ones you are training your brain. With practice, you can strengthen your ability to transition between feelings of shame and unworthiness to feelings of love and safety.

9

Healing from an Over-Identification with an Abuser

"I Am No Longer Defined by My Past"

In this chapter, we explore complex internal conflicts that tend to arise when someone has experienced childhood abuse. Long-term trauma can lead you to carry distorted thoughts and feelings about your abuser. For example, you might idealize parents who were, in reality, very hurtful. Or, you might feel as though your abuser still has control over your life. This chapter focuses on developing the boundaries that will help you find freedom from over-identification with an abuser.

"Why does my past still have so much power over me?"

"I feel overwhelmed just thinking about going home to visit my family. Part of me wants to see my parents. I miss them. But there is also part of me that feels terrible during these visits. Going home involves seeing my brother and neighborhood friends. None of them know about the chaos that happened behind the closed doors of my home. My parents were often yelling and my father would hit my brother. I felt helpless as a kid; I was never able to protect him. I still feel like I have to keep the secret, and I feel like I did something wrong! Why does my past still have so much power over me?"

Lenore came to therapy feeling a tremendous amount of shame about the abuse. She struggled with mixed feelings about both her parents. She didn't understand how her father could be so loving to her but so hurtful to her brother. She wondered why her mother never protected her brother. She was confused about why she never spoke to her neighbors or teachers about what was happening at home.

In therapy, Lenore was able to feel and validate the difficult emotions related to her childhood. She was able to recognize that she had felt betrayed when her mother didn't protect her brother. She had felt rage toward her father for hurting her brother and scaring her. The most difficult time in therapy arose when she also acknowledged the part of her that still loved her parents. This was the part of her that was willing to protect them by keeping her father's abuse of her brother a secret. She felt a deep sadness arise within her as she grieved the childhood that she had always longed for—the childhood that was stolen when her father violated her and her brother's trust in him.

As Lenore grieved her past, she was able also to recognize that her father no longer behaved abusively toward her brother. She could also see that it was not her job to keep her father's past behavior a secret. She began to speak more openly with her brother about the experiences of their shared childhood. She realized that he, too, had mixed feelings about their father and that he had been able to get support in his own therapy. She also spoke to her parents more openly about her anger and disappointment. In time, she was able to say, "I am no longer defined by my past!" These realizations allowed her to resolve her inner conflict about going home to visit her family.

Understanding Over-Identification with an Abuser

Healthy development requires that children go through what psychiatrist and family therapist Dr. Murray Bowen described as a process of asserting independence from parents. This differentiation allows you to distinguish your thoughts, emotions, and experiences from those of others. In the best of circumstances, this journey of independence is supported by loving parents who recognize the importance of this developmental stage. All children have mixed feelings toward their parents.

There will be parts of their mother and their father that they like and want to be similar to, and there will be parts that they dislike and want to be different from. Even in the best of circumstances, differentiation takes time.

The Importance of Differentiation

As we can see in Lenore's story, children who grew up in abusive households often struggle with differentiation. Children who are not differentiated are more likely to blame themselves for the conflicts and emotional challenges of parents or siblings. For example, they might feel responsible for episodes of domestic violence or carry unrelenting feelings of guilt if a sibling commits suicide. In adulthood, this can lead to tremendous emotional distress, fueling feelings of shame and self-hatred.

Part of the reason that differentiation can be difficult is that all children have an innate, biological drive toward attachment. Therefore, children will attach to parents even if they are abusive. Since there is no way to escape the abusive household, children need to make the dangerous environment tolerable. This requires a profound dissociative split between the part of the self that upholds the attachment to the caregiver and the part that holds the reality of the abuse. Often that latter part has to be cut off in order for the child to survive. Dissociative symptoms often continue into adulthood in order to avoid remembering or acknowledging the abuse.

Keeping Secrets

In some cases, children are threatened or bribed to keep the abuse a secret. In other situations, children feel an unspoken expectation to uphold the image of a "normal" family. These complex dynamics can occur whether the child is the one being abused or, as in Lenore's case, is a witness to violence against another family member. Since the child's survival is dependent upon the parents, the child tends to remain loyal and silent.

Abusive parents sometimes fear that if a child becomes independent, the child will tell others the truth about the abuse. The parents might become increasingly controlling and limit the child's contact with potentially supportive adults in the community. Additionally, the feelings of powerlessness and shame carried by the child can make it extraordinarily difficult to seek support. As the child becomes increasingly isolated, he or she is forced into further dependence upon the abusers to meet the basic needs of food, shelter, and clothing.

Please note: While this book focuses primarily on the experience of childhood trauma as related to parents, not all abuse happens in the home. Many children have been abused within religious organizations or in other community settings. Abuse that happens by a priest, teacher, coach, or other mentor can have similarly confusing dynamics for children. These abusers often spend time grooming children to become emotionally dependent upon them for their praise, attention, and guidance. A child might not want to disappoint the caring adult and, as a result, will keep the abuse a secret.

Stockholm Syndrome and Trauma Bonding

Adults who were abused as children often continue to uphold this allegiance to their abusers. This is referred to as *Stockholm syndrome*, a condition in which hostages develop loyalty to their captors and defend them, even after they have been released from captivity. Stockholm syndrome is common among survivors of long-term child abuse. It often involves a tendency by the children to defend or minimize the impact of their abuser's behaviors, such as holding loving emotions toward the abuser while simultaneously directing shame and self-blame toward themselves. These are signs that the child carries a distorted sense of responsibility for the abuse.

Childhood abuse can create a trauma bond, by which the child, out of fear, forms an attachment to the abuser. This dynamic can be reenacted in adulthood, as well. Reenactments typically occur when you haven't gotten closure from challenging your past experience. As a result, you continue to revisit the painful feelings in the hope that you can find a new, more satisfying conclusion. But without proper support, you may repeat the painful behaviors. Reenactments are often the root cause of self-harming behaviors and ongoing abusive relationships in adulthood. For example, if you have difficulty acknowledging the abuse of your past, then this might lead you to overlook abusive behaviors from adult partners. Ignoring these red flags can lead you to repeat the painful dynamics of your past in your present relationships.

Further, these distorted perceptions can lead you to have confusing thoughts and feelings about yourself and your past. You might overly identify with an abuser, leading you to become highly critical or aggressive toward yourself. In some cases, you might feel as though your abuser still has control over your life. You might have obsessive thoughts about seeking revenge, feel confused about whether or not to stay in a relationship with an abusive parent, or feel guilty when you set boundaries with an abuser.

Developing a Healthy Self

The main way to heal from an over-identification with an abuser is by differentiation. Without this healthy sense of yourself, you might feel overly concerned about gaining approval and acceptance from others, while simultaneously feeling fearful of rejection or conflict. Or, you might focus on conforming to others' needs or pleasing them. In contrast, when you are well differentiated, you are less vulnerable to being manipulated or controlled by others. You develop differentiation by exploring and understanding your boundaries, which helps you assert your separateness from others. These boundaries can also help you recognize that the voice of your inner critic or urges to self-harm are internalizations of your abusers. As a result, you can set limits with those parts of yourself.

When you successfully differentiate from an abuser, you may decide to completely separate yourself from the abuser, either because their actions were unforgivably atrocious or because they continue to be manipulative or abusive. Should you choose to stay in a relationship with someone who was once abusive, having well-developed boundaries makes it easier and safer to be in contact with that person.

According to trauma expert and author Dr. Judith Herman, healing from an over-identification with an abuser involves a grief process as you confront the painful dynamics of your family of origin. However, as you let go of your childhood longing to be taken care of, you can simultaneously increase your sense of responsibility for your life now, in which you identify your values and strengthen your boundaries. When you are aware of what is important to you, you can better stand up for your needs and focus on fulfilling your life goals.

Start Healing Yourself

In this section, you will read about Sam and Ayanna, and see how their histories of child abuse impacted their lives. The following healing strategies will focus on helping you work through an over-identification with your abuser. Your memories of how your abuser treated you might have a strong impact on how you think or behave, but remember that your past does not need to define your future. Working through this book will help you become empowered to take responsibility for your life. Therefore, I remind you that the healing process takes time, requires patience with yourself, and often calls for working with a trustworthy therapist.

SAM

"I feel like my abuser is still alive inside of me"

"I can't seem to stop replaying scenes of times when my soccer coach would manipulate and abuse me. For much of my life, I believed that I was dirty and to blame for his behaviors. The worst part is how I treat myself now. I feel like my abuser is still alive inside of me."

Sam came into therapy feeling tremendous shame. Initially, he had difficulty talking about his past. But as he felt more comfortable in therapy, he was able to open up. I learned that he had been sexually abused by his soccer coach. Initially, his coach was unusually friendly. He would send gifts to his whole family, and he began inviting Sam to watch the big games at his house. Sam shared that his whole family trusted his coach, so he was confused when his coach began to touch him inappropriately. He said that there was part of him that liked feeling special. His coach told him he was a better player than the other kids and made promises to recognize him as a star player, but he also threatened to remove him from the team if he told anyone about their "special time" together.

Sam's coach died several years before he came to see me; however, Sam's complex feelings of shame, anger, and confusion still haunted him. He told me that he both hated his coach for abusing him and hated himself for not stopping the abuse. He alternated between fantasies of revenge against his coach and feelings of debilitating shame. Sometimes he would cut himself when the feelings of shame or self-hatred were strong.

In therapy, we focused on helping Sam explore what he wished he had said to his coach. He had an imagined conversation with his coach that gave voice to the thoughts and feelings he was never able to say when the coach was alive. He also used journaling between sessions to help him move through his complex, painful feelings about the abuse. Additionally, he identified his own, internal resilience, which his coach couldn't take from him.

Through our work together, Sam recognized that his self-harming behaviors were a reenactment of the abuse. In time, his urges to hurt himself decreased. Sam had spent many years trying to make sense of events that were senseless. Ultimately, he needed to confront a painful truth—that no matter how hard he tried, he could not change his past. However, now he was able to move forward in his life.

Healing Strategy:
Speak Your Truth

As a child in an abusive household, it is difficult to have a voice. Now as an adult, you can give yourself permission to express your truth. With this healing strategy, you have an opportunity to explore any incomplete conversations or unfinished business from your childhood. Journaling can sometimes feel like a safe way to begin the healing process, especially if you feel frightened about speaking to others about the traumatic events of your past. It might be helpful to bring your written responses to therapy.

Take the time to reflect—whether in your journal, in a video, in art, or in a recording—upon what you wished you had said to your abuser. Explore any of the following prompts that relate to your history. These prompts not only address the painful impact of your trauma but also invite you to reflect upon your strengths. Remember, you can pace yourself or skip this healing strategy if it feels overwhelming for you.

- When you hurt me as a child, I felt . . .
- The worst thing that you said or did was . . .
- What I was most afraid of was . . .
- The physical impact of the abuse was . . .
- The impact of the abuse on my other relationships was . . .
- What I wish I had said to you then, but never told you, was . . .
- What you could never take from me is . . .
- I know that I am strong because . . .
- What I want you to know about me now is . . .

AYANNA

"I carried the belief that I had done something wrong"

"He told me that I was his special girl, but what he did with me was unforgivable. For many years, I carried the belief that I had done something wrong. Only now do I realize that he was the one who was doing something wrong."

In therapy, Ayanna shared her story of being sexually abused as a child by her father. When Ayanna came to see me, she carried the burden of believing she had been responsible for the abuse. She inaccurately believed that she was at fault because she hadn't said no or told anyone about what was happening, even though she knew what was happening wasn't right.

Therapy helped Ayanna to recognize that her feelings of shame and self-blame were signs that she carried a distorted sense of responsibility for the abuse. She told me that for years she believed her father could read her mind and that he would know if she told someone. Now, she could acknowledge that this was a childhood fantasy she needed to rely upon to survive, as she had nowhere else to go for support. Therapy helped Ayanna to remember that she had been just a child then. She hadn't been able to say no or to stop the abuse because she had felt frightened and powerless. But now, as an adult, she could make different choices. She began to feel compassion for herself as a little girl, telling herself that it wasn't her fault—that it never was her fault.

Healing Strategy:
Reset the Responsibility

This healing strategy focuses on remembering the fact that you were just a child and returning the responsibility for the abusive behavior to the abuser. You might find it beneficial to bring this section of the book to therapy if you find yourself getting triggered by this sensitive topic. Explore the following prompts and note your responses to these statements and questions:

- Explore any ways that you felt responsible or felt ashamed for the abuse you experienced as a child. Maybe you blame yourself because you didn't say no, didn't tell anyone, allowed it to continue, or your body responded sexually to the abuse.
- Recognize that the body is biologically wired to respond to contact, even during abusive situations. This can lead to feelings of confusion for many survivors of sexual abuse. A physical response of arousal does not equate with consent and is not an invitation for sexual touch.
- Remind yourself that you were just a child and that all children are dependent upon their parents.
- Take some time to reflect upon the reasons that a child is never responsible for the abuse. Maybe you were powerless, felt afraid that you would be killed, or you thought you were being a good child by doing what you were told.
- Take a few breaths and offer compassion for yourself for the painful challenges that you experienced as a child. Make room for any feelings of grief or loss that arise in this process.

How Am I Doing?

This chapter focused on helping you understand why you might have distorted thoughts and feelings about an abuser. While the tools of differentiation can help you strengthen your sense of self, it is common for the healing process to evoke feelings of grief and loss. Take a moment to reflect. Could you relate to the stories that were shared? Has anything in this chapter left you feeling stirred or upset? If so, remember that you can return to any of the healing strategies in this book at any time. I end this chapter with one more healing strategy to help you assert your boundaries and set limits in your relationships.

Healing Strategy:
Assert Your Boundaries

This healing strategy is focused on helping you develop your boundaries. Boundaries help you assert your separateness, an essential part of healthy differentiation. They can also help you set limits on your inner critic or self-harming behaviors.

One way to define your boundaries is to know yourself and your limits. When it comes to interactions with other people, are you willing to accept rude or aggressive behavior? How do you know when someone has crossed the line? How do you feel when someone else treats you disrespectfully? How do you feel when you treat yourself aggressively or disrespectfully? It is also helpful to know your values when asserting these healthy boundaries. Explore your values. How do you feel when you or someone else behaves in a way that is not in alignment with those values?

Here is a list of statement that represent healthy boundaries. Notice how you feel as you read these statements. Perhaps explore bringing these statements into your life to help you assert those boundaries to yourself and to others.

- I can say no, even if someone else doesn't like it.
- I can change my mind, even if I disappoint someone.
- It is not okay for anyone to humiliate me.
- I have the right to ask for more information when I am confused.
- It is okay to tell someone that I do not like how he or she is speaking to me.
- I can leave the room if someone yells at me.
- I can end relationships that are hurtful to me.
- I can tell myself to stop being so critical or hurtful to me.

10

Overcoming Feelings of Hopelessness and Despair

"I Am in Charge of My Life Now"

One of the greatest damages caused by long-term trauma is the impact it can have on your hope for a positive future. A looming sense of despair might dominate your awareness. Given that child abuse and neglect are relational traumas, you may have lost faith in other people's trustworthiness or their capacity for goodness. If you relate to these symptoms of C-PTSD, know that you are not alone. You can overcome the overwhelming feelings of hopelessness and despair by working through the pain of your past and reclaiming a sense of meaning and purpose for your life.

DARRYL

"I can't imagine a future worth living"

"I wish that I had a sense of purpose. Most days, I feel like I'm going through the motions. I wake up, get dressed, eat, and go to work. But what's the point of it all? Everything I do feels like a chore. I have no sense of direction for my life. I can't imagine a future worth living."

Darryl came into therapy seeking a sense of direction and purpose. As we explored his history, I learned that he grew up in a home where he was profoundly emotionally neglected. Both his parents were addicted to drugs and were often absent or intoxicated. Darryl's trauma was related not only to his experiences in witnessing their addictions, but also to the extended periods of time he was left alone. His childhood lacked emotional and physical connection. He learned that in order to survive, he had to raise himself. He had learned to dismiss his own emotional needs. Now as an adult, he continued to feel cut off from his emotions. As a result, his life had very little depth or meaning.

Therapy provided an environment for Darryl to attend to the ways his parents had neglected his thoughts and feelings as a child. He realized how hopeless he had felt as a child, feeling that nothing he did ever made a difference. He had been projecting this same sense of despair onto his future. In time, he became better able to validate his own feelings, and he noticed that he began feeling less "flat." Ultimately, Darryl realized that he had to take responsibility for his life.

He recognized that he couldn't take back the childhood that was stolen from him. But at this point, he could say, "I am in charge of my life now!"

Understanding the Loss of Meaning and the Rise of Hopelessness

As with Darryl, many survivors of childhood trauma experience a deep existential loneliness or sense of despair. In part, this is due to the senselessness of child abuse and neglect. C-PTSD can affect your "systems of meaning"—that is, the beliefs you hold about yourself, your relationships, the world, and your future. For example, you might believe that you are permanently damaged or that you are incapable of overcoming the obstacles in your life. Perhaps, you doubt that people can act with kindness or generosity. You might doubt that there is any goodness possible in this world. Maybe you feel a sense of despair about the state of the world. These feelings can make it challenging to find any sense of purpose, meaning, or hope for your future.

Having hope for your future relies upon knowing that your actions make a difference in the outcome of your life. As a child, you may have initially tried to make things better for yourself and your family. For example, you might have tried to relieve your parents' suffering. You may have also felt that no matter how hard you tried, nothing worked. Loss of hope often arises when you feel that you have run out of choices and there is no way to change your situation. You might feel accumulated and insurmountable disappointment or a sense of utter defeat.

The cost of despair is the loss of your vitality and your joy. You might feel bad about yourself or feel incapable of living the life that you want. Ongoing feelings of powerlessness can lead you to feel that your actions are futile. You might wonder what the point is of trying to get better or you might question whether healing is even possible. You may have grown bitter or cynical. It is essential to remember that all these feelings are symptoms; they are not signs of failure on your part. These feelings are the result of the traumatic events of your past. Most importantly, they do not need to define your future.

Feelings of despair and hopelessness can feel like heavy weights that you are carrying, in body and in mind. The healing process involves turning toward your pain and allowing yourself to feel this heaviness. Often, there will never be sufficient retribution to make up for the injustice of abusive or neglectful parents. Your pain may never be adequately acknowledged by those who injured you. Profound feelings of grief might strike you as you work through unresolved feelings of resentment or disappointment.

Remember, you do not need to heal alone. It can help to allow another person, such as a trusted therapist, to be with you in the midst of your suffering. As you allow another person to stand with you in the darkness, the two of you can learn to turn toward the light. More than anything else, feelings of hopelessness and despair benefit from unconditional acceptance and compassion. You might feel unsure about opening your heart in a world that has betrayed you, but each time you let in the gift of another person's kindness, you have an opportunity to restore your faith in humanity. Eventually, this can also help you turn toward yourself with greater self-acceptance.

Reflecting upon your relationship to meaning and purpose is another key to overcoming feelings of despair and hopelessness. Take the time to reflect on the ways you have grown as a result of those painful events of your past. Perhaps your suffering has become a source of compassion for others, or maybe your pain has inspired you to express yourself creatively. Your process of making meaning out of trauma is unique to you; nobody else can answer these profound, existential questions in the way you can.

Making meaning out of suffering involves taking responsibility for your life, here and now, by exploring your habitual thoughts and actions. For example, you might notice a tendency to think pessimistically about your life and your future. If so, you might challenge yourself to refocus your mind on positive, loving thoughts about yourself or others. It is important to keep this process realistic. When you have a history of trauma, you know that the world can sometimes be unsafe and hurtful. While it is limiting to believe that all situations are dangerous, it is equally unrealistic to tell yourself that the world is always safe and that all people are kind. But you can choose to be around people who make smart choices and who treat you respectfully. You can feel empowered to shape your future in a positive direction.

You might find that your ability to stay with positive thoughts or emotions feels limited. Here, you can imagine the metaphor of a person who has been through a famine. The person will feel sick if he immediately goes to a feast and eats as much as he can. Instead, he needs to gradually introduce simple foods and to build up a tolerance for richer, more nourishing meals. Similarly, you may need to move slowly and build up your tolerance for positive and loving feelings. With time and practice, you can bring more excitement, joy, and vitality into your life.

Start Healing Yourself

In this section, will look more closely at feelings of hopelessness and despair through Adam's and Charlotte's stories. The healing strategies in this chapter will help you focus on your strengths and your relationship to life's meaning. Charlotte's story is a reminder that healing from C-PTSD often takes time and that sometimes symptoms can reemerge, even after you have been engaged in trauma recovery for a while. If you relate to her story, be gentle with yourself, as the healing process is often not linear. Some say that healing happens in layers, as if you are slowly peeling away the layers of an onion, with the deeper parts of yourself revealed as you work down through the process. Perhaps we can also make the comparison to an artichoke—a reminder that there is always a heart at your center.

ADAM

"It's just too painful to have goals"

"It's just too painful to have goals. As a kid, whenever I really wanted anything, it got taken away. So, I just stopped wanting. Even now, I don't see the point in trying. Nothing I do makes a difference."

When Adam came into therapy, we discussed his goals for treatment. He cringed at the word "goals," letting me know that it was too painful for him to even consider talking to me about his hopes and desires. As we explored his childhood, Adam described his mother and father as mean and vindictive. He recalled times that he was excited about things as a child and how this made him a target for their cruelty. I learned then that he had very little control over his life.

Even as an adult, Adam lived a life of scarcity. He had a small apartment, with little furniture and few material items. His fridge was often empty. The times he did have something positive in his life, he felt that he had to use it quickly, before it got taken away. He would eat his food quickly, without enjoying it. He would spend money without letting himself save up for anything that he really wanted.

In therapy, Adam slowly began to open his mind to the possibility that his life could change for the better. He had lived for such a long time within a constrictive lifestyle. He attended to the grief and pain of his childhood, and he realized that he had very limited tolerance for any positive emotions. As he gained insight about his history, he could see that he pushed his good feelings away, just like his parents did when he was a little boy.

One day, I asked Adam to imagine that he had just been given a special gift. He told me that he was imagining being given a puppy, something that he had always wanted as a child. He started to feel tears well up. We both knew that the critical voices inside him would soon chime in to say that he didn't deserve the puppy, but I asked him to choose a new phrase that he would to say to himself instead. He said, "I deserve to be happy. No one can take that away from me now!" A few months later, Adam came into therapy to share the news that he had adopted a dog. His life was now focused on walking, feeding, and caring for his little friend. He could feel a sense of purpose for the first time.

Healing Strategy:
Enhance Positive Emotions

In general, human beings are wired for survival. We all have a built-in tendency to pay more attention to disturbing experiences than to positive ones, as a means of guaranteeing that survival. But when you have a history of childhood trauma, this tendency to scan your environment for threats is even stronger. Your capacity to vigilantly observe your environment was necessary to keep you safe as a child. While it is important to attend to the pain of your past, you can also learn how to offset this negative survival tendency by focusing your attention on positive emotions and memories.

This healing strategy invites you to consciously pay attention to nourishing moments that help you strengthen your capacity for positive emotions. You can do this by slowing down so you can feel and savor the experiences that evoke happiness, joy, or connection. You might notice a tendency to quickly brush off positive experiences. Instead, challenge yourself to linger in those positive feelings for a bit longer, knowing that you are growing your capacity to feel good. The following suggestions will help you enhance those positive moments:

- Take note of moments of positive emotion in your life. For example, notice when you feel hopeful, focused, calm, or connected. Allow the positive feelings to grow by actively focusing on those good feelings. See if you can stay with the good feelings for five to ten seconds, while noticing how you feel in your body.

- If someone gives you a compliment, use some time to fully receive the gift. Take a deep breath and allow yourself to let the good feeling grow. Pause and thank the person for the compliment, and notice the good feelings that arise.
- Consciously create opportunities for positive feelings. Choose to listen to a piece of music you enjoy, watch a movie that makes you laugh, enjoy a meal by savoring the flavors, or buy yourself flowers for your kitchen table. Maybe find joy in doing creative projects such as woodworking, painting, or playing an instrument, or in organizing your home or planning a trip. In truth, it doesn't matter what the task is, so long as it makes you happy. The key to this practice is in staying with the good feelings for as long as you can.
- Give the gift of kindness to others. Experiment with giving a compliment or leaving a friendly comment on a friend's social media post. Notice how you feel during and after the experience. Explore how it feels to offer a random act of kindness to a stranger—say, by extending a smile or opening a door for the person. In what ways are you nourished by the experience of giving? Allow yourself to attend to any positive emotions and sensations for just a little longer than you normally might.

CHARLOTTE

"Shouldn't I be over this by now?"

"Even though I've been in therapy for years, I can still get triggered. When this happens, I start to feel utterly hopeless, like I will never get better. Shouldn't I be over this by now?"

When Charlotte began therapy, she had debilitating depression. She had been hospitalized on several occasions for depressive symptoms, including considering suicide. Her history of sexual and emotional abuse had profoundly impaired her trust in people. However, she was dedicated to developing better coping strategies. During therapy, she began to notice steady improvements in her psychological well-being. She felt increasingly connected to other people and has even begun writing a book, in the hope that her experience might help others who have faced trauma in childhood.

Recently, Charlotte came to our session feeling very upset. She had had an argument with a friend, who then abruptly ended the friendship. This experience brought back difficult feelings of abandonment and loneliness. Charlotte revisited the old feelings of being a burden, and she told me she thought she was just "too much" for anyone to handle. She felt hopeless and started to question whether she would ever be healthy.

I shared with Charlotte that it is normal to feel sad and hurt when we have been rejected by another person. Together, we attended to the grief that arose as a result of her conflict with her friend. We reflected upon the fact that growth is often not linear, and that it is common to experience setbacks during the healing process, especially when they are triggered by current events. I also reminded Charlotte of the overall growth and healing that she had achieved.

Charlotte understood that she was revisiting feelings that were related to her traumatic past. But instead of being critical about the return of her symptoms, she recalled how she had in the past developed the skills to attend to her pain with compassion. As a result, she felt more connected to her inner resilience, more determined than ever to write her story, and she was able to resolve her distress relatively quickly.

Healing Strategy:
Reflect upon Your Strengths

Growing up with a history of childhood trauma can lead you to focus on your pain and problems, while simultaneously ignoring the ways you are strong and resilient. A strengths-based approach to healing involves focusing on your positive qualities. This helps to counter the difficult feelings of hopelessness or despair when they arise. Take some time to write your answers to the following questions in a journal. Notice how you feel mentally, emotionally, and physically after focusing on your strengths.

- What positive qualities best describe you? (For example, you might explore how you are a caring person, a good friend to others, have a good sense of humor, believe in fairness, or enjoy spending time learning new things, including a willingness to read and engage in the activities in this book.)

- Reflect upon your growth. (For example, what are the positive changes that you have created in your life as a result of your commitment to healing? What strengths have you discovered about yourself?)
- What did you learn as a result of your healing process? (For example, perhaps you opened up emotionally, discovered a new spiritual perspective, or explored a new creative capacity. Or, maybe you have realized your capacity to be brave, determined, or mentally tough.)
- What hopes or visions do you have for your future? (For example, what new qualities would you like to expand and grow? What goals would you like to set for yourself? What do you need to do to accomplish these goals? What do you need to support you to be successful?)

How Am I Doing?

As we come to the end of this chapter, reflect upon how the emotions of hopelessness or despair can show up in your life. Could you relate to the stories that were shared here? Has anything in this chapter left you feeling distressed? It is important to remember that there will be times in your healing journey when you need to build your resources and focus your attention on your strengths. At other times, you will want to attend to your emotional pain. The healing strategies in this book are meant to support both of these intentions, and both have their value.

The final healing strategy in this chapter explores the role of grit and its relation to growth. Grit is a powerful reminder that our most significant achievements are the result of our willingness to stay engaged in challenging experiences. This is very much true when it comes to trauma recovery.

Healing Strategy:
Grit and Growth

Grit is a key to success in many aspects of life, and in terms of trauma recovery, it is a reminder of the value of determination and perseverance. Examples of grit are choosing to learn something new even though it is challenging or dealing with difficult experiences instead of avoiding them. Research on grit reveals that what facilitates your capacity to embrace challenge is the ability to observe your impulses without immediately seeking gratification. This capacity for self-control helps you stay with discomfort longer. In trauma recovery, it is grit that helps you stay engaged in the difficult process of working through your pain.

Reflect on experiences of grit in your life and explore how you might nurture your own grit. Take some time to review these questions and statements and write about them in your journal.

- As a "survivor" of C-PTSD, in what ways have you engaged in life even though you have felt afraid?
- Recall a time when you asserted yourself or used your will. How did it feel to stand up for yourself? How did you feel afterwards?
- How have you been able to get back up when life has knocked you down? How were you able to persevere and overcome setbacks in your life? What or who has helped you access your strength in difficult moments?
- In what ways are you engaged in learning something new in your life?
- When you notice a desire to do something on impulse, such as eating one more cookie than you actually want, take a moment to pause and reflect. Stop and notice how

you feel in your body as you mindfully experience the delay. Does this change your interest in the action you were about to take?

- Reflect on how you approach tasks in your life. Notice if you tend to jump from one activity to another. If so, can you challenge yourself to completely finish one task before beginning the next?

11

Keep Up the Momentum

Psychologist and author Rollo May wrote, "Courage is not the absence of despair; it is, rather, the capacity to move ahead in spite of despair." This reminds us that it takes profound determination to stay engaged in life, especially when you have C-PTSD with a history of childhood trauma. Since the healing process is not linear, you may still experience times when you are more acutely aware of the pain of your past. Therefore, it is valuable to view the healing process as a marathon, not a sprint. Most importantly, by using these healing strategies on a regular basis, you can strengthen your resilience. This not only helps you respond to distressing symptoms more quickly and effectively but also it will help you expand your capacity for joy.

Moving Forward

As we come to the final chapter, I invite you to reflect upon the gains you have achieved as a result of your commitment to healing. You might notice that your inner critic has grown quieter, giving you greater access to a sense of peace in your mind and body. Perhaps you notice that you feel more compassionate toward yourself, or that you identify less with the shame and burdens of your childhood wounds. Maybe you notice a greater willingness to trust others, or you are able to be a kinder and more loving friend. You might notice that you can handle increasing amounts of stress with confidence and ease. Or, you might find that it has become easier to assert your boundaries when you need to.

The burdens of trauma arise not only as thoughts and emotions but also as patterns of tension in the body or restrictions in the breath. So, we cannot think our way out of our symptoms. The healing strategies in this book have guided you to feel and move your body in order to restore a sense of freedom, and I invite you to remember that these somatic practices are most effective when practiced regularly. Perhaps, in working through the strategies, you notice that it feels easier to connect to your body or that you feel less dissociated. Maybe you also notice that you are responding more effectively to distressing sensations and are less likely to become flooded with emotions.

I invite you to remember that it is common for parts of you to hold the emotions and memories related to traumatic events. These parts may have helped you separate from your pain in order to survive. The strategies in this book have focused on showing you how to strengthen your awareness of your adult self, grounded in the here and now. When you are connected to your adult self, you are more likely to feel clear-headed, in tune with your intuition, and in touch with your inner wisdom. As a result of the practices in this book, you may notice that it has become easier to create nurturing or reparative experiences for the painful memories of your past.

Overall, as you take note of these signs of healing, I hope that you can see that your efforts are helping you grow stronger. With practice, you can develop greater faith in your capacity to return to a growth-oriented mindset and to have hope for your future. In time, you might notice that you go for longer periods of time when you feel balanced, grounded, and connected to your life.

What to Do if You're Still in Distress

Healing from trauma doesn't mean that you will no longer experience times of emotional distress. In fact, you may need to accept that, no matter how hard you try, some of your symptoms will persist. This is not a sign of failure on your part; it is a reminder that the effects of complex trauma are often profoundly layered and held deep within the mind and body. Remember that reclaiming your life from childhood trauma requires a long-term commitment to yourself and to the healing process. My hope is that this awareness can help you reconnect to self-compassion, rather than leave you feeling discouraged or hopeless.

Think of this book as a resource during times when you are experiencing distress. Now that you are familiar with C-PTSD and some healing approaches, you may have chosen some strategies that have been the most effective for you. Additionally, you may have found specific passages that helped you feel hopeful. Mark these pages so you can revisit them as often as you need, and return to these practices when you know that you will be facing a stressful situation.

Remember, the deep work of reclaiming yourself from complex trauma involves the careful guidance of a therapist. A book cannot replace a compassionate and well-trained counselor. We are not meant to walk the healing path alone. Since childhood traumas are relational wounds, having a positive experience of a healing relationship can help restore your faith in the goodness of other people. In time, therapy can help you build your capacity to hold yourself and your pain lovingly.

If you have found it difficult to find a trauma-informed therapist to work with in person, remember that we live in a time when we can access a wider range of support systems. You may be able to find a therapist who will work with you remotely. In addition, you might explore joining a support group for trauma survivors in your local community. There are also several C-PTSD support groups online. Look for groups that have clear rules supporting respectful communication. Participation in well-run forums can reduce feelings of isolation and shame and can help you realize that you are not alone.

Closing Thoughts

Recently, I was walking through a park. I noticed that there was a muddy path that crossed a flowering meadow. Heavy foot traffic had created this pathway, damaging the grasses and flowers. Now, on both sides of the meadow, there were ropes and a sign said the park officials were rehabilitating the field. They had planted new seeds and kindly requested that visitors stay out of this section of the park to allow for the reparation and new growth. Visitors were directed to a beautifully constructed wooden walkway to enjoy the meadow without creating harm.

This is a powerful metaphor for healing—a reminder that we must restrain ourselves from walking the well-worn, trampled path created by a damaging past. The ropes serve as a boundary that we cross when we allow self-critical thoughts or hurtful actions. The sign represents how we must set limits with ourselves to reduce behaviors that cause harm. We must practice staying off this well-worn but ultimately unwanted path in order to allow for new growth. We *can* create beauty, even in places that have been damaged. And we must create a new pathway—one that allows us to enhance our capacity for joy, warmth, compassion, and love.

What seeds are you planting? What new path are you ready to walk?

Resources

These are some resources for your continued healing of complex PTSD and childhood trauma. Keep in mind as you seek help that some of these sources will resonate for you and others may not. Choose the ones that feel supportive for you and that align with your own beliefs and values. Also, remember that online forums are not always well regulated. Because of the painful nature of complex PTSD, some sites might include content that is unfiltered and may be triggering. Pace yourself by choosing carefully what, when, and how much content to expose yourself to in order to avoid feeling traumatized again during your healing process. Trust yourself: If it doesn't feel good to you, turn instead toward the resources that feel healing and supportive.

Complex PTSD Informational Websites

CPTSD Foundation, developed by Athena Moberg: Find compassionate support through daily recovery support calls, free support groups, blog, and join the Facebook page for positive recovery messages. https://cptsdfoundation.org

Healing from Complex Trauma and PTSD, by Lilly Hope Lucario: Explore extensive resources, including guidelines for finding the right therapist and a blog, and join her Facebook page for a supportive discussion with other C-PTSD survivors. https://www.healingfromcomplextraumaandptsd.com

Out of the Storm: Find resources about treatment and recovery from relational trauma, engage in their online support forum, and read their blog. https://www.outofthestorm.website

Beauty After Bruises: Find valuable information for family members and partners supporting a loved one with C-PTSD, resources for survivors, and a blog. https://www.beautyafter bruises.org

PsychCentral.com: Use their search engine to find relevant articles about C-PTSD and childhood trauma. You can find online community forums here as well.

TraumaSurvivorsNetwork.org: Informational website with online support for survivors and their loved ones

Help Finding a Therapist

The following websites offer search engines to help you locate a therapist near you. In the United States, teletherapy (online psychotherapy) must be provided within your state. If you are seeking telehealth psychotherapy, expand your search to include therapists in your state who may not be within driving distance but could still be accessible to you.

International Society for the Study of Trauma and Dissociation (ISSTD): https://isstd.connectedcommunity.org /network/network-find-a-professional

International Society for Traumatic Stress Studies: https:// istss.org/public-resources/find-a-clinician.aspx

EMDR International Association (EMDRIA): https://www .emdria.org/page/findatherapistmain

Psychology Today: http://therapists.psychologytoday.com /rms/prof_search.php

Theravive: http://www.theravive.com or use their telehealth provider finder at http://www.theravive.com/therapists /e-counseling.aspx

Crisis Hotlines, Text, and Chat Lines

National Domestic Violence Hotline: 1-800-799-7233

National Suicide Prevention Lifeline: 1-800-273-TALK (8255)

National Network: 1-800-SUICIDE (800-784-2433)

Self-Harm Hotline: 1-800-DONT CUT (1-800-366-8288)

GLBTQ Hotline: 1-888-843-4564

Trans Lifeline: 877-565-8860

Crisis Text Line: Text "DESERVE" TO 741-741

Lifeline Crisis Chat (online live messaging): https:// suicidepreventionlifeline.org/chat/

References

Bowen, M. Lanham. *Family Therapy in Clinical Practice.*
Lanham, Maryland: Jason Aronson, 1993.

Brach, T. *Radical Acceptance: Embracing Your Life with the
Heart of a Buddha.* New York: Bantam, 2004.

Cloitre, M., Courtois, C. A., Ford, J. D., Green, B. L.,
Alexander, P., Briere, J., & Van der Hart, O. (2012). "The
ISTSS expert consensus treatment guidelines for complex
PTSD in adults." Retrieved from https://www.istss.org/
ISTSS_Main/media/Documents/ISTSS-Expert-Concesnsus
-Guidelines-for-Complex-PTSD-Updated-060315.pdf

Courtois, Christine, and Julian Ford. *Treating Complex
Traumatic Stress Disorders (Adults): Scientific Foundations
and Therapeutic Models.* New York: Guilford, 2013.

Fisher, J. *Healing the Fragmented Selves of Trauma Survivors:
Overcoming Internal Self-Alienation.* New York: Routledge,
2017.

Goleman, D. *Emotional Intelligence.* New York: Random
House, 2006.

Hanson, R. *Hardwiring Happiness: The New Brain Science of
Contentment, Calm, and Confidence.* Easton, PA: Harmony
Press, 2016.

Hayes, S. C. *Get Out of Your Mind and Into Your Life: The New
Acceptance and Commitment Therapy.* Oakland, CA: New
Harbinger, 2005.

Herman, J. *Trauma and Recovery: The Aftermath of Violence—
From Domestic Abuse to Political Terror.* New York: Basic
Books, 1992.

Kerr, M. *Bowen Theory's Secrets: Revealing the Hidden Life of
Families.* New York: Norton, 2019.

Knipe, J. *EMDR Toolbox: Theory and Treatment of Complex
PTSD and Dissociation.* 2nd ed. New York: Springer, 2018.

Levine, P. *In an Unspoken Voice: How the Body Releases Trauma and Restores Goodness*. Berkeley, CA: North Atlantic Books, 2010.

Levine, P. *Waking the Tiger: Healing Trauma: The Innate Capacity to Transform Overwhelming Experiences*. Berkeley, CA: North Atlantic Books, 1997.

Linehan, M. M. *Skills Training Manual for Treating Borderline Personality Disorder*. New York: Guilford, 1993.

Maddi, S. R. *Hardiness: Turning Stressful Circumstances into Resilient Growth*. New York: Springer, 2013.

Maiberger, B. *EMDR Essentials: A Guide for Clients and Therapists*. New York: Norton, 2009.

McGonigal, J. *SuperBetter: A Revolutionary Approach to Getting Stronger, Happier, Braver, and More Resilient*. New York: Penguin, 2015.

Ogden, P., K. Minton, and C. Pain. *Trauma and the Body: A Sensorimotor Approach to Psychotherapy*. New York: Norton, 2006.

Ogden, P., and J. Fisher. *Sensorimotor Psychotherapy: Interventions for Trauma and Attachment*. New York: Norton, 2015.

Rosenberg, S. *Accessing the Healing Power of the Vagus Nerve*. Berkeley, CA: North Atlantic Books, 2017.

Rothschild, B. *The Body Remembers: The Psychophysiology of Trauma and Trauma Treatment*. New York: Norton, 2000.

Parnell, L. *Attachment-Focused EMDR: Healing Relational Trauma*. New York: Norton, 2013.

Paulsen, S. *When There Are No Words: Repairing Early Trauma and Neglect from the Attachment Period with EMDR Therapy*. Scotts Valley, California: CreateSpace Independent Publishing Platform, 2017.

Porges, S. W. *The Polyvagal Theory: Neurobiological Foundation of Emotions, Attachment, Communication, and Self-Regulation*. New York: Norton, 2011.

Scaer, R. *The Body Bears the Burden.* 3rd ed. New York: Routledge, 2014.

Schauer, M., and T. Elbert. "Dissociation Following Traumatic Stress: Etiology and Treatment." *Journal of Psychology* 218, no. 2 (2010): 109–127.

Schwartz, A. *The Complex PTSD Workbook: A Mind-Body Approach to Regaining Emotional Control and Becoming Whole.* Berkeley, CA: Althea Press, 2017.

Schwartz, A. *The Post Traumatic Growth Guidebook: Practical Mind-Body Tools to Heal Trauma, Foster Resilience, and Awaken Your Potential.* Eau Claire, WI: PESI Publishing, 2020.

Schwartz, A., and B. Maiberger. *EMDR Therapy and Somatic Psychology: Interventions to Enhance Embodiment in Trauma Treatment.* New York: Norton, 2018.

Schwartz, R. *Internal Family Systems Therapy.* New York: Guilford, 1997.

Seligman, M. E. P. *Authentic Happiness: Using the New Positive Psychology to Realize Your Potential for Lasting Fulfillment.* New York: Atria Books, 2004.

Shapiro, F. *Eye Movement Desensitization and Reprocessing (EMDR) Therapy: Basic Principles, Protocols and Procedures.* 3rd ed. New York: Guilford, 2018.

Shapiro, R. *Easy Ego State Interventions: Strategies for Working with Parts.* New York: Norton, 2016.

Siegel, D. *The Developing Mind: How Relationships and the Brain Interact to Shape Who We Are.* New York: Guilford, 1999.

Van der Hart, O., Nijenhuis, E. R., & Steele, K. *The haunted self: Structural dissociation and the treatment of chronic traumatization.* New York: Norton, 2006.

Walker, P. *Complex PTSD: From Surviving to Thriving: A Guide and Map for Recovering from Childhood Trauma.* Lafayette, CA: Azure Coyote, 2013.

Index

Acknowledgments

I would like to thank a few key people who have been essential to the writing of this book. First, I would like to thank Callisto Media, Rockridge Press, and my editor, Seth Schwartz, for their vision, support, and guidance in this project. Thank you for making this resource available to individuals with C-PTSD, their loved ones, and the therapists who support them. I feel grateful to my mentor, Betty Cannon, for her ongoing compassionate presence and guidance in my life. Lastly, I am deeply and most profoundly grateful to my family for their love of me and their support of my work in the world.

About the Author

Arielle Schwartz, PhD, is a licensed clinical psychologist, EMDR therapy consultant, certified Clinical Trauma Professional, certified yoga instructor, and internationally sought-out speaker. She lives and runs a private practice in Boulder, Colorado. She earned her doctorate in clinical psychology at Fielding Graduate University, and she holds a master's degree in somatic psychology from Naropa University. Ms. Schwartz is the author of three previous books: *The Complex PTSD Workbook: A Mind-Body Approach to Emotional Control and Becoming Whole* (Althea Press, 2016), *EMDR Therapy and Somatic Psychology: Interventions to Enhance Embodiment in Trauma Treatment* (W. W. Norton & Company, 2018), and *The Post Traumatic Growth Guidebook* (Pesi Publishing, 2020). She believes all people deserve to be empowered by knowledge and is dedicated to offering informational mental health and wellness updates through her heartfelt presentations, social media presence, and blog.